Almost
Thence
Sum

Almost Thence Sum

Jeffrey Herrick

AFTERWORD BY
Jerome McGann

Station Hill Press
BARRYTOWN, NEW YORK

Published by Station Hill Press, the publishing project of the Institute for Publishing Arts, Inc., 120 Station Hill Road, Barrytown, NY 12507, New York, a not-for-profit, tax-exempt organization [501(c)(3)].

Online catalogue: www.stationhill.org
email: publishers@stationhill.org

Acknowledgments:

"Grave Waves" appeared in *The Antioch Review* (75: 4) 2017, with particular thanks the editors.

Front Cover: Jean-Léon Gérôme, "The Almeh with Pipe," 1873, public domain.

Back Cover: Ian Heywood et al., SARAO, 2022: MeerKAT radio image of the heart of the Milky Way. Special thanks to the observatory for permission to publish here.

Library of Congress Cataloging-in-Publication Data
Names: Herrick, Jeffrey, 1946- author.
Title: Almost thence sum / Jeffrey Herrick.
Description: Barrytown, NY : Station Hill Press, 2023. |
Identifiers: LCCN 2022037733 | ISBN 9781581772210
Subjects: LCGFT: Poetry.
Classification: LCC PS3608.E7745 A78 2023 | DDC 811/.6–dc23/eng/20221014
LC record available at https://lccn.loc.gov/2022037733

Printed in the United States of America

Contents

FOREWORD   9
Poetrying My Own   9

Almost   17
Almost   17

Thence   69
Get Bach   70
Jussive Fruit   73
Lines from a Lost Folio, Recently Exhumed in London   75
Reflexions   77
O Penned Sesame   82
Fin Hoarse Meres   84
Repeat   87
Poetrying   92
How to Read a Poem   95
Loaded Words   97
No Such Agency   101
Slow Light   103
Heart o Art   105
Un   107
Wots in a Paronym?   109
Scotography   111
Quadrate Probe   113
Hyades to Hades   116
祝詞   118
Auscult   120
Hygiantics: Musicology and Philology   122
Aqua Vitae   124
Elected Affinities   127
Air de cours   129
Linear Near   131

Sum   133

Do the Math   134

A Decade o Roundels   136

Calculus   146

Atomic Number One   148

The 4% Premonstration   149

Accretion Discs   150

Grave Waves   152

Rigmarole   161

Prime Rime   164

AFTERWORD
Jerome McGann   165
Jeffrey Herrick's Verse: Compositions of the Flying Hand   166

SELECTED HERRICK BIBLIOGRAPHY   179

ABOUT JEFFREY HERRICK   180

ABOUT JEROME MCGANN   180

Almost
Thence
Sum

for Mitsuko

Poetrying My Own

I

I try to make poems that listen to themselves, so that readers may do the same. This is connected to pater Pater's patter about all art aspiring to the condition of music, and to my own sense of sound sound sounded, as all of creation is a matter of vibration, reverbed as Om. Poetry calls attention to our languaged condition. Language is a system of constraints, as is music, "sound grammar," as Ornette Coleman put it and played it. Poetry tries this out with its emphasis on reflexive techniques, such as rhyme and rhythm. Free verse and free jazz are not free, they just refocus boundaries.

I try to make poems that acknowledge and push boundaries at the same time. Each poem is an epistemological and ontological exercise. I try, for example, to see how much a sonnet can hold. I typically do this by making it one sentence, a "unit of thought," as I was taught to call it in grade school. How far and how deep can I go? I try to make each poem psychedelic, a research engine. In "Oming" I tried as many sonnets as Shakespeare for the sake of earing spheres his little wist, weirds, as "words without thoughts never to heaven go." To get closer to that, I moved on to longer units of my own device, first 24 lines. By "By the Numbers" I mean the demeaned means to try the sigh of what math hath in score for our store of lore, the hero: zero, a rondo of centuries and censures, arts and sciences, sequences and consequences. Of "Anything you say..." I say that *Absalom and Achitophel* endures beyond the pall of the political because of the agenbite of Dryden's wet wit, the justice of language meant, not languishment. In "Skeltonic Tonics" I seek sonic sooth to soothe toxic talk. In "Almost" I post all I can of bliss missed, a narrative of errative grammar after glamour, art after parts. For my own parts, I next tried 48 lines, or fathoms, 144 feet long, sentenced to life when read aloud. This is the pith of "Lith," a connection and opening, a Mozartian start at a consideration of birds and angels in relation to spoken and written language, with deliberately slow chromatic melodies exploring the extent to which "hope" is a sing with feathers.

I try to make poems in which language lives, even as it reveals itself as a sign of alienation. A rose by any other name would smell as sweet, but Juliet certainly wanted another name. For Gertrude Stein a tautology made do. But when we try to be precise about roses, we turn to Latin, that so-called dead language, for a taxonomy of economy. When I make poems, I look things up, and I try to make things sing. Saying "It's Greek to me" just means being too lazy to look things up. The Greeks do that, too, displacing their laziness as Chinese. Pound chose to foreground both Greek and Chinese, an opening I embrace. When I use Greek, I seek polysemic seams. We get "ode" from ἀοιδή, but in the original it also means song, legend, tale, and story. Yes, I want all those sings, not just praise, except for just praise.

I try to make poems that root for their roots. I use epigraphs and notes and marginalia. I avoid translations of any sources that show any sensitivity to sound sounds, for there is no such sing, or else I make the point with traducements on display. Language engages and disengages us. Poetry tries to make this predicament its antepredicament, sound logic in deed. Poetry tries itself. Poetrying is a harkening of darkening, an event horizon, a zone of Choronzon faced as fate. Poetry gives the game a way to show it was lost from the first. It is radically honest in its lays of lies, as Byron knew. This is the opposite of trumped up tongues in power plays. Poetry forces us to face our goat song, τράγος ἀοιδή, with our tragus, as a comedy of earers. It hears our diction of contradictions, our ʾaḍdād[1] addlement.

I try to make poems that face a crisis of language, a world of the word as a commodity for flattening and deadening to a dead end in demon dement, or as a bludgeon for dumbing and numbing us down to unheard community, a meeting in assured surdity to the pathos of meaning on the path to meaninglessness. I intend to attend to this vortex, O as the sound of a recognition of cognition, as the round of a zen enso, an essential null, as the moan of an open closure, as as displays displacement. Readers may want to chide me, as the nurse does Romeo — "Why should you fall into so deep an O? — or they may want to ride along. Of course I pun, as Someone once said poets should, because the cracks track the light into the black whole. And I allude to nutter ludicity and uttered seriousness, an echo a choice *morceau*.

I try to make poems in which the use of languages other than English reinforces the force of the sings. Do I have to defend this after Joyce and Pound? What does attention to the tension in tense and declension in late Latin or early Greek not have to do with the universal grammar of music? This is also personal: I have spent most of my life as an alien among alien tongues. I have tried to learn; I want to know and show as much about the world and the word as I can, the sounds and rounds in my head and heart.

I try to make poems that seek their truth in beauty, that rare thing, as Ornette Coleman put it. I aim to imagine the music of the spheres, to ear dearer mirrors of dire errors and higher airs.

---

1. Arabic أضْداد (plural of ḍidd, ضِدّ = "a word that has two contrary meanings"), words which, according to the definition of Arab philologists, have two meanings that are opposite to each other, e.g. the verb bāʿa which may mean "to sell" and also "to buy" (= ishtarā); even the word ḍidd itself belongs to the same category of words, for in such an expression as lā ḍidd a lahū it has not the meaning of "opposite," but that of "equal."

II

Lith

To limn limbs o aspen
Pen *Populus tremuloides*

With Laplace transformed to Pravuil
εἶδος, ἀοιδή o お出で　　　　　　　　　　[oy day] वेदस् [vedas]
image　　*song, story*　　*coming, going, being somewhere*

In the lith o arith o lithes
O lēoht in the leaves qui vive

In vivâ voce ploce,
Utter mutter o flutter,

Subtle scuttlebutt o flux
　　　　O λευκός os so *sonor*
　　shining

Zoner phones loan
Oms through loam and rhizome

To phloem for tomes o gnomes
O genomes, homes o Horus

For us to suss in dust,
As Osiris is risen to myth,

With Lilith, from regolith to otolith,
Hear here, the lumière

From seer o lyth in lid,
Lede led to red

　　　　　　　　　　赤い糸

Thread read in said
Lied, the lay o the and

In the lore o or, the score
For ores in scoriae, stories

O aureate stiction, fictions
O gangue o gongorismo y argot

Begot for gongs gone
In luciphorous logolepsy, babel-

Icious ἰχθῦς ἰσχῦς —
     fish, fool   power
Else ixnay is the say o pray

Told untold rhymes
Ago in the lowball lobo

Dictionary, nary an airy
Oboe for ſos to behold

Over depths o dolt debt,
A race to disgrace place

And pride, lyin' a lien
On mien and gleaner o keens

In dull lulls o unmulled
Whines, signs o lines

Cut to robot retweets
As bitter as *Endzeit* insights

O the kenned in the canned, a scand
O old English as ish

Supplants the kith and pith   γιγνώσκω
O wordsmith, the keys to seize

The qi and glee in trees,
The esprit o core ichor.

Remembering:

Such wild warblers in
Needleless larches must be
Visionary saps.

~~~~~~

Line-item Vet o O o Otolith

Is lith a limb for joint property with a gate open to symmetrical calls o 0? Is it a myth for a time that is out of joint, like Malory's lady, Nymue, with Pellinore, king of Listenoise?

> and ye shalle be welcome said Pellinore to the Courte of kynge Arthur
> and gretely allowed for your comynge and so he departed with the lady
> and brou3t her to Camelot
> Soo as they rode in a valey it was ful of stones
> and there the ladyes hors stumbled and threwe her doun that her arme was sore
> brysed and nere she swouned for payne
> Allas syr sayd the lady myn arme is oute of lythe wher thorow I must nedes reste
>   me
> ye shal wel said kyng Pellinore
>   -Le Morte Darthur III, iii

2 Is *Populus tremuloides* apt, as accurate as Latin for a time a tremulous populace is displaced?

3 At such a time, can a real variable convert to a complex frequency, as Laplace placed himself to become a recording angel, a Parvuil that prevails in writing and righting songs?

4 Is it acceptable to use sounds from Japanese for the coming, going, and being somewhere in the oy day, oy vey, when knowledge, vide "veda," is marginal?

5 Can we count these numbers that go and suffer?

6 Is the light of old English in my pen and pun on aspen, the tree I'd rather be buried under than Hardy's yew?

7 Do my sounds echo the quality of those leaves, a repeat reaped in rhyme, never in identity?

10 Can sounding these leaves leave a mouth bright, shining, joyful?

12 Can we learn the language of trees? Can we communicate as well as they do? Can attention to linguistic roots serve as effectively for survival? Cf. Thoreau, Wohlleben, Simard.

14-18 Can myths and hieroglyphs of bird brains lift ours, Lazarus-like, the dead read in heard light?

19 Can the light in lyth be an etymon, a true lead to visionary airs?

20 Can "we the lede" lead readers to heed the hum of the human, the ply of a people like a tepal?

21 Can we read red threads, bloodlines, in Japanese the ties of fateful love?

22-23 Can I lead readers to sprechgesang, as they say, as they say this song?

24-28 Is this diction recondite? Can oxymorons help us find light in blight? If I indite to indict mindlessness, do I not need to lead readers to mind what is lost in gongorism gone, to revel in revelations of spurred rays in wordplays that place the florid against the horrid?

29 Can sounding out contradictions in Greek roots be a route to religate us to seek to speak religion trued, to moor us to more?

30 Can pig Latin help us twig flattened real sings?

32-33 Can we, with Lincoln's ken, repudiate the wolf's dictionary, liberate "liberty" from white supremacy? Is this allusion lost? Do you vote for a footnote?[2]

34 Can we hear in the woods (*hautbois*) winds to carry the day to a way to a high lo that trumps the trumpets of trumpery?

43-44 Do you hear my fear that English has become dumbed and numbed in inexactitude, a scandal in a minced oath?

45 As the Greek I know for "I know" peeks in from the sidelines, can you hear counterpoint?

47 Need I repeat that the key to qi is air, 气, that *elan vital* needs sing?

48 Can we saps sing our way in myth to divine kith and pith?

Can you forgive me for recycling my own haiku, since it echoes the point at the end and serves as a transition to the birds in the sequence?

2. Abraham Lincoln, April 18, 1864: The shepherd drives the wolf from the sheep's throat, for which the sheep thanks the shepherd as a *liberator*, while the wolf denounces him for the same act as the destroyer of liberty, especially as the sheep was a black one. Plainly the sheep and the wolf are not agreed upon a definition of the word liberty; and precisely the same difference prevails today among us human creatures, even in the North, and all professing to love liberty. Hence we behold the processes by which thousands are daily passing from under the yoke of bondage, hailed by some as the advance of liberty, and bewailed by others as the destruction of all liberty. Recently, as it seems, the people of Maryland have been doing something to define liberty; and thanks to them that, in what they have done, the wolf's dictionary has been repudiated.

Almost

፩

በአልማዝ

bäʾalmaz
on-Almaz

በሩን

bärrun
door-def-acc

ዘጋሁባት

*zäggahu-**bbat***
I closed **on her**

I closed the door on Almaz (to her detriment)

Amharic Denominalizing suffixes:
-*änña* – *hayl-änña* 'powerful' (from *hayl* 'power'); *əwnät-änña* 'true'
(from *əwnät* 'truth')
-*tänña* – *aläm-tänña* 'secular' (from *aläm* 'world')
-*awi* – *ləbb-awi* 'intelligent' (from *ləbb* 'heart'); *mədr-awi* 'earthly'
(from *mədr* 'earth'); *haymanot-awi* 'religious' (from *haymanot* 'religion')

The grammar of a descant on descent
Can't scant cant

Or decent dissent, no spent
Men renewed by news

Of glamour in the clamor for grimmer
Glimmers of the golden untold

In pre-Homeric home, a hymn
To hum Om and moan

Of lairs of liars as desires
Sire sighs the size

Of *I*s eyed in seizures
Of *amour propre,* the prop

Staged as ramage damaged
And word deterred from terra

In lunes that croon no runes
Or rouns, only rounds of unsound

Device, the vice of syntax
Tracked to lacks of lux

In silver slivers of verse
That reflect wrecked recks

Of unearthly worth unearthed
Without mirth in dearths of curses

As ears borne to biers
Carry airs as cares

And fare where dares are truths
Too rued to voice a choice.

ב

ὅπου ὁ σκώληξ αὐτῶν οὐ τελευτᾷ, καὶ τὸ πῦρ οὐ σβέννυται

where their worm dieth not, and the fire is not quenched

Mark 9:44

As unleavened loaves left
Her bereft, Almaz, amazed,

Almost froze but rose to unclose
The door, the horror of more

Perception, register of rejection
Of the lie of life as psi,

Lifted leavings as cleaving
And leesing the lease of the word

To trow drow as the throe
That glozes eros in erose

Oneiros with onerous arousals
Of ruses as cues to burdens

As clues to loose the music
Of heres as sheer presence,

A presense of postliminal lumen,
A room to moor her mirror

And quire the fire as dire
Hands fan ire

In epistrophes of sophistries, sinister
Insisters sans history, her story

As begot by *Gott* or goat-
Man, demeaning meaning

إله Until *El* spells hell   אל
To tell fell tales.

21

ג

For Almaz prayer bared
Error, pared air

To snared rum drum
Squared to despair, not the hum

Of homed opening to hope
In acoustics that stick in the spirit,

Lit from split to knit
Wit as writ in fyttes

Of peeks at bleak chouses
That rouse no αvατριχιάζω or anas   *goosebumps*

Of sanity but hear tears.
Almaz wept. The swept

Tempi of temples of simple
Samples of jangles that entangle

Ruptures of raptures capture
Od audience to read

Muses as ruses but abut
The music of sick psych

When numb pneuma mourns,
The morn owning singing

In spheres nearing clear
Circles of eterne turned

To discern the rhyme of time
With prime chimes of the sublime.

ع

And, after all, what is a lie? 'Tis but
*   The truth in masquerade; and I defy*
Historians, heroes, lawyers, priests, to put
*   A fact without some leaven of a lie.*
The very shadow of true Truth would shut
*   Up annals, revelations, poesy,*
And prophecy—except it should be dated
Some years before the incidents related.
*   -Byron, Don Juan, Canto 11, xxxvii*

Lost lots of lays
Lie with worms in terms

Time dates, ever
Late to state the plain

Pain that phased Almaz
Minus phrase, the frame

Of the nameless that with Spenser "writ
No language," leesing wit   *per Ben Jonson*

With twitterverse bits of nonce
Sense deaf to clefs

And claves that bend ears
To near verities and fair

Prayers in airs that translate
Late tales of O

Played as clade-made melodies,
Lodes of modes that die

In eigenvectors, sectors of specters
Where no truer weirds

Were ever wrought, the plot
Sought in soughs as the surcease

Of susurruses in Hesperus were oestrus
For Almaz to muse upon, the uterus

Of humor in peripeteia an anagnorisis   插科打諢
Of ecesis in the diegesis of Lachesis.

⌒

por las amenas liras
por las amenas liras
y canto de serenas os conjuro
que cesen vuestras iras
y no toquéis al muro,
porque la esposa duerma más seguro.
  -Juan de la Cruz, Cántico Espiritual

Bewildered in the wilderness, to build
On nihility Almaz almost

Lost the host of numbers,
No obstante, tarde para la ira,

Here she read the wall
As writing, citing the light

In nightmares that flare to square
The garden and pardon calembours

In *retruécanos* trued in amphigories
To give the game a way

With seraphic sapphics to traffic
In glossolalia that glosses lays

To say the play to the stage
Where sheerer earers near

Clairaudiance of Od in the gods'
Aposiopesis, to pause and piece

Together a *pas de dieux*
That does a Blake dance

On the sands of ands to add
Almaz to the ἀγγελοι that amaze

26

El alma y cantar mala   माला
To la-la a lama or mullah   མོལ་ / مَوْلَى

Can count to *contes* of haunts
To chaunts a *baxajuan* owns.

ר

The forest rests on chorist
Mycorrhizal rhythms that rise   *220Hz*

To airs and bear roots
To stoors that store the lore

Of the plan of elan for recitals,
As aspens and beeches teach

The reach of spirit when tirrits
And tears tear the ear

From Shakespeare to here as Almaz
Muses on the mazes of the way

To say yea in play
That stays the woods and woulds

Of words with *sourd* surds
As swords to slay lays,

A world dulled in loud
Crud, a shroud no oud   عُود

Or ode leads to threnody,
The end rendered in deadened

Hum, drums of sums
On a road of accounts in the unread,

The rood a door to movies
"Based on a true story,"

Almost always an awful
Sign, no trine design.

٧

אֲרָרָט

Ἀραράτ

At Ararat the art Almaz
Almost ghosted hosted

Her nearer to Noh, not Noah,   熊
With *gagaku,* not a gaga God   雅楽
                                                  elegant music

Dogging disobedience in dense
Invective and vindictive directives,

The error of terror a horror
Sans ors in more amor

So the mood of doom makes room
For moors in scores with cores

Vorstellung tongues to sung
Numbers that unnumb when come

To the diaphoresis of diaporesis as Isis

Decides the lied of the deeds

Of the dead and unread, the red

赤い糸

Thread

heard
  in the heart

In parts

leading the voice
To choices on precipices with auspices

In pieces that feeze mondegreens
And eggcorns to seize seas

As gees in ha-has with laws
Of minced oaths whose troths

To Thoth as thought evince

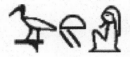

The mother of orthometry met.

٨

Where are you now? Who lies beneath your spell tonight?
Whom else from rapture's road will you expel tonight?
-Agha Shahid Ali
O ravishing disunities

For Almaz a ghazal was a gaze   غَزَل
At razed days raised

To says of يَأس as yes   *yas: despair*
In iterant irritants in instants

Tense with witness in fits
Of peeks at textspeak that wreak

Wrack to rack and crack
Case in inflections to reflect

On 音楽 in talk with Bach   *[on gaku] sound enjoy=*
Back on track backwards   *music*

As *canon cancrizans* can scan   *Dan*
Lines to fine finds   *Tepfer*

Of Gold-Bug crypto scripts
On kryptonite in apocalypto nights,

The plight of light in inverse
Verses versus universes

Of blight in the rorrim, the rim
Of mere more, crores   करोड़

Of lakhs as lacks track   लाख
Black wholes that house

32

Bleak Greek: ἔσχᾶτος,
Toast, as scat tones

On lorn words norn
Ghost hosts of O.

፱

Bid me to weep, and I will weep,
While I have eyes to see;
And having none, yet I will keep
A heart to weep for thee.

Bid me despair, and I'll despair,
Under that cypress tree;
Or bid me die, and I will dare
E'en death, to die for thee.
-Robert Herrick, "To Anthea, who may command him anything"

If Amharic accidence damned
A door for Almaz, Ur-uncle

Bob robbed the reaper,
Won now and how,

O pun, o eye, with a way
To say more for amor

Than sore eros, the algolagnia
In language a gauge of the gain

In pain in the pathos of an antispast,
The scalding ring of catadioptric

Tracks of rhythm and rhyme
An anabasis of katabasis, a basis

Of truth in jhuth, sound   झूठ
Sound, veracious chicane,

Eman in name that rises   إيمَان
From rose to sweet sum   *faith*

34

Things that sing numb
Numbers to come to the Ingdom

Of Be, as Βὔβλος, the source
Of papyrus, put the word on the world,

And the psalmistry is history, a story
Of scores as core lore,

Tone notes of note
For the pneuma in neume and name.

And whosoever hath seen thee, being so fair,
Two things turn all his life and blood to fire;
A strong desire begot on great despair,
A great despair cast out by strong desire.
-Algernon Charles Swinburne, "Hermaphroditus"

The hex of sex vexes
The heart, a hurt that circles

Back to attack the tracker
Of truth in ruth rhetoric,

The theater of toric anaphorics,
Dysphoric forms for Pythagoras

Or Archimedes to meet in defeat,
The calculus of fulcrum come

To an angle an angel embrangles,
The first cause a clause

As subjunctive as that that
Almaz almost were,

A law of the wal that saw
Life was, elif   *else if*

The conditional condition, a rendition
Rending the ending in a pending

א   ألف

Ring of the plight of lingo
Trying to go from nil

To أَلْفُ لَيْلَةٍ وَلَيْلَةٌ
ʾalfu laylatin walaylatun

Then annul an annulus in us   *A thousand and one nights*

As dust with lust, modulus
Nonplussed in modes as codes

Of volatiles trial tales
Of vapor trails as grails.

And every motion, odour, beam and tone,
With that deep music is in unison:
Which is a soul within the soul—they seem
Like echoes of an antenatal dream.
  -Percy Bysshe Shelley, "Epipsychidion"

Deep clepe of soul
Tholes the whole hole

Of אֱלֹהִים, lo, hum   Elohim
Of him who holds gold

Logs of phantom limns
Of almosts as عالمة of Almaz   almas

Phrase phases of essays
To say ineffable pessimals

Define the lines of जीव   jivas
From jive and archive of נֶפֶשׁ   نَفْسَ
                                                     nephesh

In meta M psychosis,
Osmosis of cosmos to mos,

Unless morceaux meld melody
And emmeleia to more so mores

Respire the pyre and promise
Of Prometheus, the us to suss

In entanglement with the angels of imagination
In an unholy hylozoic and etheric

Lyric of oneiric elasticity,
Site of Γαῖᾰ and ⌐   *Gaía*
                                               cross

Cognizance of the sex of intertext
In the laws of form that morph

To swal lows of ॐ,   *om*
A realm of ψαλμός os.   *Psalmos*

١٢

what Door
Is that, sculptured in elfin freak?
The portal of the Prince o' the Air?
Thence will the god emerge, and speak?
El Deir it is; and Petra's there,
Down in her cleft. Mid such a scene
Of Nature's terror, how serene
That ordered form. Nor less 'tis cut
Out of that terror—does abut
Thereon: there's Art."
"Dare say—no doubt;
But, prithee, turn we now about
And closer get thereto in mind;
That portal lures me."
-Herman Melville, Clarel II, 30

Read diurnal numbers
As portals toll and tell

Ways to say the day,
A labyrinth with abatjour for hyacinth,

Not adamantine amaranth, perianth
As a synth for forms of orifices,

Ora pro Almaz, mused
To hyaline lines in signs

That sound grammar to more
Than doors and harm, to harmolodic

Ludics, the music of the heres
That disappear, as will Shakespeare,

In vanishing ravishing with singing
That amazes and blazes in blazons

Of zones of O, the flow
That goes and knows the los

Behold no paroled roles
Save waves or M-

Dimensions, the declension of tension
And tense past recension, as sense

Of hence and whence mense
The almost as the host of hosts,

The ghost post of the coast
Of quondam, numb and dumb.

Cf. Edmund Spenser, *The Fairie Queene* III, iii:
the learned Merlin well could tell
Under what **coast** of heaven the man did dwell

١٣

The night of nought brought
The lot of ether to either

Or or neither, nether
Theres or Erewhons, — the One

Done, the other Un —
An apparent horizon a zone

Of horrisonous nouslessness and loss,
As light fights Zeit

Unto geist until no story
Were, satori a satire

On significance, the immanence of Silenus
A silliness of oblivious idiocy,

Delirious gossip as gospel,
The spell that malingers to mingle

And linger in lingual squalls
Of misconstrual, as qualia call

Esse est percipi,
Desipience is science, the resiance

Of sighs and seizures *du jour*
To see and say nirvana,   निर्वाण
                                                blown out

Nay, may nocturnes turn
To Chopin and Lu Ban   魯班

And build cloud ladders
To nebulae that be as Almaz.

١٤

Pour dire vrai, je crains que ta coquetterie
Ne trouve pas un prix digne de se efforts
Qui, de ces coeurs mortels, entend la raillerie?
Les charmes de l'horreur n'enivrent que les forts!
  -Charles Baudelaire, "Danse macabre"

Amazed in a maze of paraphrase
Almaz almost o ghost,

A lay allays no nay
In illecebrous douce danceuse

As nous looses loss
O soul, less pneuma

Than neume loomed to doom,
A modal mood, as wert

Words ere airs pared
Their fare to prose poses,

Plus or minus roses,
Ere reverencing references

To personal journal and pronomial
Hymnals with banal annals

Of limbic nimbs as limns
For corona vires vitae

Or mighty me memes,
When dervishes serve devices

Beyond fond bond
That trick ichor from dhikr   ذِكْر

And loan stones koans,
Songs of long circuits

Sorted in torques of *mort*
To trom-bone sones.

閑さや岩にしみ入る蝉の声
-松尾 芭蕉 [1]

1. *In stillness drilling into granite cicada shrills*
   -Matsuo Basho

44

١٥

Castalia is the name of that fount in the hill's fold,
the sea below,
narrow beach.

Templum aedificans, nor yet marble,
"Amphion!"
-*Ezra Pound,* Canto XC

This is not a drill
Or a rock, this trill doc

Clocks mock stochastic
Periastics in stichs that tick

Talk to tone poem
In oneiromantic antic drum-

Time to emit a rhyme
For pulse and appulse sans occults

ॐ   Of *om* homed in *on*   音
楽   *Gaku* gods who square

Organs in circles of oracle   *Organ²/ASLSP*
Auricles, hear heart   -*John Cage*

In O and consonant avowals
Of the lot wot to tow

The line to the Nine, to Helicon
And back, to track acts

Of recreation to creation and black
Immaterial as lives gyve

The soterial irreal to ethereal
Theories of atomic wait,

The pause that refleshes as the maws
That laniate light go right

About, as Almaz causes Amphion
Clauses in ambient entia.

Guiding our imaginations by that omniprevalent law of laws, the law of periodicity, are we not, indeed, more than justified in entertaining a belief—let us say, rather, in indulging a hope—that the processes we have here ventured to contemplate will be renewed forever, and forever, and forever; a novel Universe swelling into existence, and then subsiding into nothingness, at every throb of the Heart Divine?

And now—this Heart Divine—what is it? It is our own.
        -Edgar Allan Poe, Eureka: A Prose Poem

To coax from hoax an X,
Go to Poe and face

The music, a mirror to ear
A ⌐ across to gloss

Os as so, the quo
Qua crow of manifest

O in lo beheld
In contradictions and fictions, reckoning

Dead read as said,
Plumbing dumb and coming

To tongue wrung to sung
Rungs to ring Greek   κινέζικα

Calends and end endings,   αλαμπουρνέζικα
Call the all graal,   这对我来说实在难以理解

Gravel the grave and rave
Evermore of double Dutch

In pig Latin, twig
The big ricture, an aperture

For sure grasps of gasps
And trows of the throes of rapture,

Language the gauge of rages
To stage sage Almaz

As alma, almost host
Of heaven, "I am that I am."   יהוה
                    ד ד = ד

۱۷

> *The cup...crosses itself? Inscribes a stark*
> *Twinbladed axe*
> *Upon the block, sideways? Is it the mark*
> *That cancels, or the letter-writer's kiss?*
> *The X*
>
> *Of the illiterate?*
> *Fulcrum and consort to our willowy &?*
> *The space of a slow breath indrawn,*
> *Simplicity itself, it waits and then goes on*
> -James Merrill, *The Changing Light at Sandover* (493)

As tautology teaches a rose
To rise and pass the smell

Test, so tsem-is-is a tension
Between belief and Dis,

This signifier the signified
Deixis, "simplicity itself,"   *almost Almaz*

"Depending upon what the meaning
Of is is," as is

O, cusp o abyss
Or clasp o vis viva

Sound sounding a round
Figure, like π, the psi

O *qi aquí a chi*   氣
Keys in the code for nodes

That bode odes to *sedo,*
"I allay," "I stay," to say

The biology of ambilogy, a palilogy
O O-ologies,[2] a circle to cercal

Hora, hora, hora,   Ὥρᾱ, होरा, הוׂרׇה
Ouroboros course to torque

Cercueil to credulous dulce,
The pulse nonfalse in pulsar

But nonplussed in suss of dust,
Trusting in just gravitinos.[3]

2. Cf. William James, Postscript to The Varieties of Religious Experience:
"The ideal world, for [refined supernaturalists], is not a world of facts, but only of the meaning of facts; it is a point of view for judging facts. It appertains to a different '-ology,' and inhabits a different dimension of being altogether from that in which existential propositions obtain. It cannot get down upon the flat level of experience and interpolate itself piecemeal between distinct portions of nature, as those who believe, for example, in divine aid coming in response to prayer, are bound to think it must.

3. The gravitino field is conventionally written as $\psi_{\mu\alpha}$ with μ = 0, 1, 2, 3 a four-vector index and α = 1, 2 a spinor index. For μ = 0 one would get negative norm modes, as with every massless particle of spin 1 or higher. These modes are unphysical, and for consistency there must be a gauge symmetry which cancels these modes: $\delta\psi_{\mu\alpha} = \partial_\mu\varepsilon_\alpha$, where $\varepsilon_\alpha(x)$ is a spinor function of spacetime. This gauge symmetry is local supersymmetry transformation, and the resulting theory is supergravity.

Reach me a gentian, give me a torch!
let me guide myself with the blue, forked torch of this flower
down the darker and darker stairs, where blue is darkened on blueness
even where Persephone goes, just now, from the frosted September
to the sightless realm where darkness is awake upon the dark
and Persephone herself is but a voice
or a darkness invisible enfolded in the deeper dark
of the arms Plutonic, and pierced with the passion of dense gloom,
among the splendour of torches of darkness, shedding darkness on the lost
bride and her groom.
-D. H. Lawrence, "Bavarian Gentians"

The declension of O goes
To albedo O and back

To black hole of soul
As Oceanus Procellarum "alarum

Macbeth I, ii

Within" mins of Min,

An oxymoronic tonic of *Jin*,

人   神

Figure of E=mc²
And *vis viva voce*

Conserving O as one
And all and all as none,

Ω as mega maker
Of A apographa of plasma,

Astral ravel Almaz
Muses upon until almost post,

51

A prolonged melodic note
Among moving harmonic notes

At the end, a *duenda* in *a*
Cappella, a selah for candela   סֶלָה

For photopic tropic tone
Proem from keen green

Ken on to ink and skia-
Graphy, from graphite to graphene

And carbon nanotube ebons,
Allotropes of Plutonic tonics.

۱۹

*We were right. Helen herself denies an actual intellectual knowledge of the temple symbols. But she is nearer to them than the instructed scribe; for her the secret of the stone-writing is repeated in natural or human symbols. **She herself is the writing.***

> *I was not interested,*
> *I was not instructed,*
> *nor guessed the inner sense of the hieratic,*
>
> *but when the bird swooped past,*
> *that first evening,*
> *I seemed to know the writing,*
>
> *as if God made the picture*
> *and matched it*
> *with a living hieroglyphic*
> *-H. D., Helen in Egypt, "Eidolon" II, iii*

The pith of myth herewith:
Almaz was as is

Is, a way to say
Si, si, to see

Double, babble and bible,
Scribble and sibyl in time,

Rhyme of abyme minded,
Ecco! Ecce imāgō   यम

As ghosts go and post
Liminal figurae for prefigural

Epigraphs as fragments contingent
On Amon, *mon* of *nom*   門 *(gate)*

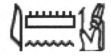

De dieu disclosed as os,
O *torii* for story o transitory   鳥居 *(gate)*
                                              bird abode

ἀποκᾰλῠψῐς on lips as spell
O *spil* for Hamlet, gambit

For musical chairs, spares
O *parō,* "I prepare," "I learn

By heart," "I purpose," "I provide"
Kami tree, key   神 *(god)*

To *chair chère* shared
In air *clair,* no prayer,

A gathering, rather, of matter
In cyphers of aether teachers.

A Door just opened on a street —   [Door] there opened — to a house —

1 — lost — was passing by —

An instant's Width of Warmth disclosed —

And Wealth — and Company —

The Door as instant shut — And 1   [as] sudden

1 — lost — was passing by —

Lost doubly — but by contrast —

Informing — Misery —   enlightening —• enabling — [Misery —]

-Emily Dickinson, unbound sheet

The testament of detriment, meant
Or demented, in door or rood,

Pauses Almaz and chouses
The word as a drow shadows

Sad gods of gaps
That sap aporias to dysphorias

As stories of scorias, the scores
Of goat songs, wrongs   τράγος ῳδή

Wrung to devices of sacrifice,
Guillotines in the skenes as keens

For capitulated or belated prate
Grate *da da capo* as Gestapo

Modes drone, the phones
Of the human pneumon no pneuma   πνεύμων

55

Renews, blue slews
To imbecile resile, the trial

Anacharsis wis wisted,
The abyss bid, vis

Inertiae for reliquiae or fasciae
In unfascicled minutiae of moment,

Torment pent in meter
Hymns limn for phantom

Tomes on tombs as rooms
That almost open in puns.

٢١

Neutrals collected bones

or journeyed behind on foot

shouting at invisible doors

to open.

There were guards who approached

stealthy as linxes

Always fresh footprints in the forest

We closed a chasm

then trod the ground firm

I carried your name

like a huge shield.
-Susan Howe, *"Chanting at the Crystal Sea"*

Just saying is just
Skywriting minus justice,

The words blur to blurbs
With verbs that pervert and reverb

In retweets and retreats, in cowardly
Lyin lines, the likes

Of conspiracy theories sans queries,
Superspreader events of demented

Ending in dead and unread
Minds, blind to binds

The maligned and demeaned, quarantined
In disjunctive subjunctives, strive

To survive, as vindictive invective
Prevails, and the avail of velleities

Pales to the beyond, the demimonde
Of Almaz, whose cause is the almost

That trues muses on glossology
In chrestomathies of pasigraphy to pass

Along numbers that unnumb, songs
Strong against wrongs gone

To embolalia with qualia unqualified
To yield shields or field

Ergodic prosodics for melodic
Universal wavefunction junctions.

ὔμμες πεδὰ Μοίςαν ἰ]οκ[ό]λπων κάλα δῶρα, παῖδες,
cπουδάcδετε καὶ τὰ]ν φιλάοιδον λιγύραν χελύνναν·
ἔμοι δ᾽ ἄπαλον πρίν] ποτ᾽ [ἔ]οντα χρόα γῆρας ἤδη
ἐπέλλαβε, λεῦκαι δ᾽ ἐγ]ένοντο τρίχες ἐκ μελαίναν·
βάρυс δέ μ᾽ ὀ [θ]ῦμος πεπόηται, γόνα δ᾽ [ο]ὐ φέροιcι,
τὰ δή ποτα λαίψηρ᾽ ἔον ὄρχηcθ᾽ ἴcα νεβρίοιcι.
τὰ ⟨μὲν⟩ cτεναχίcδω θαμέωc· ἀλλὰ τί κεν ποείην;
ἀγήραον ἄνθρωπον ἔοντ᾽ οὐ δύνατον γένεcθαι.
καὶ γάρ π[ο]τα Τίθωνον ἔφαντο βροδόπαχυν Αὔων
ἔρωι φ. αθειcαν βάμεν᾽ εἰc ἔcχατα γᾶc φέροιcα[ν,
ἔοντα [κ]άλον καὶ νέον, ἀλλ᾽ αὖτον ὔμωc ἔμαρψε
χρόνωι πόλιον γῆρας, ἔχ[ο]ντ᾽ ἀθανάταν ἄκοιτιν.
]ιμέναν νομίcδει
]αιc ὀπάcδοι
ἔγω δὲ φίλημμ᾽ ἀβροcύναν, …] τοῦτο καί μοι
τὸ λά[μπρον ἔρος τὠελίω καὶ τὸ κά]λον λέ[λ]ογχε.
     - Cαπφώ[4]

As woman to women, Murasaki
Shikibu, like Sappho, focuses

On twilight sones, sounds
The O zone o pathos, the almost

O Almaz, *che fosse stata*
Stato di dichiarazione condizionale,

The condition of the word, the fiction
In diction, the striction in lines

Of affliction, as dereliction licks
The marginal, the nominal, the penetralia

Of Gödel incompleteness, gods
Gone on no known

Noun or lown, owned,
Aux absent les os,

In nullibiety lullabied in rimose
Rimes rhythmed for sphygmo-   σφῦγμός

Phones for loan *mon*   文
For love letters to fetters,   恋文

Sorts of shrove catachreses
Devoved to eisegeses for phoresis

Of lies with lyres, mimesis,
As is this, of a Hilbert space

Everted to face the phase
Shift o schesis and diathesis.

4. Cf.
Josephine Balmer:

The gifts of the Muses are violet-threaded,
rare: follow their path, my daughters, pursue
the lyre's clear-voiced, enthralling song.
Once I, too, was in tender bud. Now old age
is wrinkling my skin and my hair is turning
from black to grey; my heart is weighted,
knees buckle where I danced like a deer.

Yet what else can I do but complain?
To be human is to grow old. They say
Eös, the rosy-fingered dawn, whispered,
of love to Tithonus, whirled him away
to the very edge of the world, beguiled
by his youth and beauty. Yet still he aged,
still he withered, despite his immortal wife.

Anne Carson:

You, children, be zealous for the
beautiful gifts of the
violetlapped Muses
and for the clear songloving lyre.
But my skin once soft is now
taken by old age,
my hair turns white from black.

And my heart is weighed down
and my knees do not lift,
that once were light to dance as
fawns.

I groan for this. But what can I do?
A human being without old age is
not a possibility.

There is the story of Tithonos,
loved by Dawn with her arms of roses
and she carried him off to the
ends of the earth

when he was beautiful and young.
Even so was he gripped
by white old age. He still has his
deathless wife.

J. Simon Harris:

Hold on, little girls, to the beautiful gifts of the violet Muses,
and cling to your love of the clear sweet lyre, that lover of music.

My skin was once supple and smooth, but now it is withered by age;
my hair had been lustrous and black, but now it is faded and gray.

My heart grows heavy; my knees, too weary to stand upon,
though once, they could lift me and dance, and could leap as light as a fawn.

I grumble and groan on and on—and yet, what else can I do?
No woman has lived without aging, no man has eternal youth.

They say that Tithonus was held in the rosy arms of Dawn,
who carried him off to the ends of the earth, so her love would live on.

Though charming and young at the time, and despite his immortal wife,
he too would succumb to old age in the end of his endless life.

Yet, thinking of all that I've lost, I recall what maturity brings:
the wisdom I lacked as a youth, and a love for the finer things.

And Eros has given me beauty not found in the light of the sun:
the passion and patience for life that so often is lost on the young.

Lachlan Mackinnon:

Live for the gifts the fragrant-breasted Muses
send, for the clear, the singing, lyre, my children.
Old age freezes my body, once so lithe,
rinses the darkness from my hair, now white.
My heart's heavy, my knees no longer keep me
up through the dance they used to prance like fawns in.
Oh, I grumble about it, but for what?
Nothing can stop a person's growing old.
They say that Tithonus was swept away
in Dawn's passionate, rose-flushed arms to live
forever, but he lost his looks, his youth,
failing husband of an immortal bride.

Edwin Morgan:

Girls, be good to these spirits of music and poetry
that breast your threshold with their scented gifts.
Lift the lyre, clear and sweet, they leave with you.

As for me, this body is now so arthritic
I cannot play, hardly even hold the instrument.
Can you believe my white hair was once black?

And oh, the soul grows heavy with the body.
Complaining knee-joints creak at every move.
To think I danced as delicate as a deer!

Some gloomy poems came from these thoughts:
useless: we are all born to lose life,
and what is worse, girls, to lose youth.

The legend of the goddess of the dawn
I'm sure you know: how rosy Eos
madly in love with gorgeous young Tithonus

swept him like booty to her hiding-place
but then forgot he would grow old and grey
while she in despair pursued her immortal way.

Martin West:

[You for] the fragrant-blossomed Muses' lovely gifts
[be zealous,] girls, [and the] clear melodious lyre:

[but my once tender] body old age now
[has seized;] my hair's turned [white] instead of dark;

my heart's grown heavy, my knees will not support me,
that once on a time were fleet for the dance as fawns.

This state I oft bemoan; but what's to do?
Not to grow old, being human, there's no way.

Tithonus once, the tale was, rose-armed Dawn,
love-smitten, carried off to the world's end,

handsome and young then, yet in time grey age
o'ertook him, husband of immortal wife.

٢٣

Farewell, my lute!—and would that I
Had never waked thy burning chords!
Poison has been upon thy sigh,
And fever has breathed in thy words.

Yet wherefore, wherefore should I blame
Thy power, thy spell, my gentlest lute?
I should have been the wretch I am,
Had every chord of thine been mute.

It was my evil star above,
Not my sweet lute, that wrought me wrong;
It was not song that taught me love,
But it was love that taught me song.

If song be passed, and hope undone,
And pulse, and head, and heart, are flame;
It is thy work, thou faithless one!
But, no!—I will not name thy name
   -Letitia Elizabeth Landon, "Sappho's Song"

Eulalia, the name in the lay
Of the lyre, quires as dire

A dearth as "deep in earth"
Appended to "Eulalie" rends   *Poe*

Ends to lies of psi
That pry *bona fides*

From bones bemoaned to tell   εὔλαλος
Well, like L.E.L., the fell

Knell of the alma[5] omega,
A Z of *shi* as sies

　　　　　　　　　　　　　　　　　詩 (*poetry*)

　　　　　　　　　　　　　　　　　死 (*death*)

In seas of tares, resets
Of galaxies to etymons of O

γἄλᾰ　　　　　　　　　　　　　κύκλος

صَفِرَ　　　　　　　　　　　　　शून्य

As all is almost, a holey
Ghost post accoasted

In hoys convoyed in nomoi,　　　νόμος
The laws of saws and swas[6]　　spā

As old as English tolled
To ish as nether threne

For thoughts taught to lie,
As in "too deep for tears,"

Unless seer ears bear　　　　*werdʰh₁om
Biers here to hear

Almaz clauses in the jaws,
The ossicles, the cochlea, the labyrinth.

---

5. See Jean-Léon Gérôme, "The Almeh with Pipe":

عالمة

عَلِمَ

6. Cf. **swā swā** iċ ǽr sǽġde

　　as I said before

Perhaps some saints in glory guess the truth,
Perhaps some angels read it as they move,
And cry one to another full of ruth,
"Her heart is breaking for a little love."
Though other things have birth,
And leap and sing for mirth,
When spring-time wakes and clothes and feeds the earth.
-Christina Rossetti, "L.E.L."

As *triste improvisatrice* triced
Solum from noumenon to *nom,*

Almaz is gauze as concause
Sourced to segue fugue

State to state *états*
D'esprit à rebours, a Des Esseintes

As saint of second sights,
Apostle of apostils, angel

Of owl mirrors, nearer   *eulenspiegel*
To queer quire of lyre

Trued to disquietude when occluded
Than when kenned and penned

In plain pain sites,
Reflections of abjection in reboations,

Latrations of tralations that traduce
By a grimmer grammar in the clamor

For more doors to close on others
Than in any other levers

δος μοι που στω και κινο την γην

Of deceivers that sever gravity
And levity, brevity and longevity,

Via *vis mortua,* outro
As the other is othered as authored,

A spirituosity of cecity and surdity,
The utmost minus the almost.

Thence

Get Bach

The line twixt nit-twit
And knit-wit twists from knurl

O null to kneel at knell
O nous sought sans sense

O surd sounded, not a knot
In pronunciamento, audience o Auden,

Rather in rathe, wroth
Writhes with wry wraiths

That fife dumb fiefdoms
Into spellbound fugues yous

Can use to moo muse
O *om* home in MUD

Mood for od odes,
Yields to abet alpha

Waves toward beta beats
That mete the meta o theta,

The hertz o hacker humor,
Or more on low laws

Ohm meets in resistance
From musicians at omega, that mega

O whence M, thence Ω,
As conductors wend wands

In winds toward toward rewards,
To wit, ears near seer

*For years musicians
have been told that the ear
Is able to separate
any complex signal into a series
of sinusoidal signals—that
It acts as a Fourier analyzer.
This quarter-truth, known
as Ohm's Other Law,
has served to insure the distrust*

Spheres where spells, here
Mhos o seminal semes

O Ss as sybilants sow
So attic antics, urges o demi-

Mound relic, radiation
Still rife in sheets

O reeves o glassed gas
As asses force gees

From ha-has, awes from Blake
Dances dunces purl,

O grate prise, to raze
Rays that yet read

Metered feet panted
Into a cororner, nary a wrong

Fellow, yet every sing you say
Canned and willed unwonted

Shall be used in a quart
O raw agains, u-

Turns into nought mares,
Mere ur-urges, unless anisotropic

Tropes pick isotropic eyes
To rhyme rhythm with O°

K range horizon, sones
Event science sighs

At in near misses, darling,
Buds o maybes underheard,

*with which perceptive musicians
regard scientists, since it is
readily apparent to them
that the ear acts
in this way only under
very restricted conditions.*
        -W. Dixon Ward,
          "Musical Perception"

71

Overhead unknown unimagined,
As IT takes angel intelligence

To balance the uns o universe   運
In verse, book a loom

From glooms beyond gamma
Lays in lies trued

To rounds o unnumb numbers   *CMR=2.725*
As oss o tongues, read

Shifts o ifs in f-
Stoppered ark dark

Merlin rouge o makers
Up amongst angsts

From the word gone, ward
O writ warts, o *fahrts*

O parts, arts o erred
Airs, raree fees

Unpaid, bereft footed
Unto sign o segno, get Bach 𝄪

Jussive Fruit

The heft of the haft of an exclamation,
Mark, breaks to a period

Period! that halves haves
Into noughts, not, note,

As commas of twined identities
In sharp flats, sound

Abodes, of course, but in coursed
Tongues, those coarse vehicles

In voids vacations avoid,
Homed in on hohlraum articles

Particle physics abhors
For topoi no known bosons

Or typos could swear on as bosuns,
Un less see or say,

運

Say, as aphasia's a phase
For a phrase away in pasigraphy,

A chrestomathy of mythed tips
With change on the way. This

Way out, pleas, and donut
Forget your valuables, as values

Bank from knab to gab
In lines that bear their own

Cognation in cognitions of quillets
Larfing all the whys,

The quality of the qualia the lair
Of liars in implications, the imprecations

Of witch, would wake finnikins
In printers and gain hieroglyphic

Flexibility, point out zombie
Arguments, the phones of the I-podded,

And launch elenchs that clinch
Fits in the pores of aporias,

As if if were not
Abstracted!, for the *f* of the ineffable

Starts stops that socket
The buzz of zero over

To uwies that keep you
In Ur discomfort zone,

The home of the pome that tempts
Attempts to the poems at the end

Of the mined in mind, the minah
That stands descants and delivers

The runes of ruins, the cull
Of the vild in play pens。

Lines from a Lost Folio,
Recently Exhumed in London

Act III, Sc. vi
Capulet's orchard

Juliet: I know Romeo's not as brave or bright
As I, and rough his way as is this bar
Of cherry, no vessel worthy of waves or evasion
Whose base I slump at, in pale wonder, impaled
By the uncouth ferule the taut untutored youth
Applied to me—how like this trunk—and how
Abruptly his fumbles dribbled, the sheets already
As red as these plucked fruits from his fingers.
All fruits are as tasteless to me now as the putrid
Concoction the guileful friar hath filtered to enchant
This phial with numb abstractions. I'm of half a mind,
As I'm a fractioned and factioned maid, to make
A Lesbian leap to the burdensome comforts of verse
And the dulcet fortunes of tenderer breasts, like those
Of Nurse, yet more ardent and less witless,
As my cousin Rosaline offered when she came
With a gentler kiss to my chamber but a fortnight
Ere I manned my mannikin for paltry flight.
Alas the lacks I see on second thoughts,
Rendering this falsifying draught a truer bitter
Sweetness than it would have were this world
Other than I'll find should I awake from wake.

Nurse: These trees blind me but stop not my ears,
And what I hear here turns my troubled blood
From banished bumpkin to a city of licit lights
In a namesake she'd take were she not so naughty and
          haughty.
I've ridden the wrong horse, as is my wont;
I want, anon, to find one that would serve
To transport the old bones to nether ecstasies.

Juliet: My will to quaff this here, as full as empty
Folly in its tide, betides a haste that wastes
What chance of cousined love remains to cozen

From time and man; I'll abide to tell the cock's-crow
Of mortal plans in Artemis' mondaine wit.

Reflexions

Tongues tarter than saucy,
Their musical muscle yet sung

Of, the stung unable to stable
Their stallions of gallant errancy,

Clio turned to Melpomene
To ask the meaning of this.

—A demonstrative pronoun, relative,
Here of no deity deictic,

Fool, but as full of sense
As sound for who has ears.

—Is it then reflexive?

—A bit be bitter

But rhyme has reason,
As all flaws season

Flows from blows to blues,
Which my sighs sing.

—You suffer suffering lightly,

A cause for curses at me,

The atramentous tremendous onus
On us who lie enscrolled

To school schlemiels to meet
Their makers, those masquers who mark

Us up to gelastic costs
Of jealousy and cerebrose sub rosa

Cerebration that hums like your
Hamlets through om to omen.

—Men're amenable to amen.
If you spit at spats, brat,

You'll not startle Aristotle,
But you'll ablute catharsis,

Sis, to a diluted and dilated
Nullity, a nihil aisle

To isles mere seats of deceit.
Excreta meet for meat.

—You sieve abuse and never
Save, serve vengeance

For benevolence, your lens but
To incinerate the late and left.

—And you'd have the labors of simple
Simian scribblers as ductus

To tape records for gibber.
Gibbets be bitter bits;

Let cursive curse as durst
Rarest airs for pairs

Of unamused muses such as moronic
Sophomores flush to flesh

Out outré contrivances
For coherence when here entoblast

Lasts as long as wrongs
Called to culled and cold

Rights lights serve
Transparently to shadow to shades.

—Neither dumb nor dim
Were you ever, sis,

To suss how we be
Patterns of patter over splatter,

Bloodless nun-beings
For ravening scrivenery that rages

For order in ordured ordeals,
Ideals irreal as relief

In leaves left to fall
On exes exacted in axes

Of blood that flood fields
With bubbles and babel from Babylon

On and on, off
Your automatic acroamatic scale.

—Full fallen from your eyne,
Mine twin, twined

In theory to practice acts
Of rehearsal for hearses and hoarse

Plays that pun to punish
Any of many that mayn't

Sing to ring the singed
Fringes of dungeons of dudgeon,

The umbras of umbrage that raze
The ages to sure erasures.

—Be we Calliope?
Nay, ever nigh

Melody in memoriam I'm
Pressed to sense progress

In rests when step by stupa
Stops sign sciences;

Insights see into
The means to the end, the rent

Chromaticism schismed by silence,
The old by absolute cold.

As tropes of entropy we entrance
The exit strategy of energy

As one mirror turned
To another, a dance of diminuendo

Recursions in catoptromantic pairs,
As maples duple and dapple,

Doppelgangers to stipple simple
Rhymes to prime sublime

Reflexions tell time's
Clitic inflexion's a transit

As we be to ward
A world in words which bewitch

The echo of cool from cruel
And eye Is to ice

Inured to ataxia and attacks
Of oxymorons such as common sense.

—This is that: signa:
Sing to sign *signe*

To sapience, nous to loosen
The noose we impart to depart.

O Penned Sesame

For the parse that refleshes, be,
Obeah, a tree of rife

Rives by definition, as war:
The human mania to die

For lies. Nay, the lays
Of the lands demand metonym-

Psychosis, paralipomena lips
Mean in metaphosphors for amphi-

Bology of biology in special
Palinodes for paligenesia of epicrises

In anamnesia, the elysia of esthesia
On sees of ex cathedra exed,

Crossed in epodic episodes
No I-podded replicant can

Follow in autos epha,
Graphs that raft shallow

Sheols and abandon Abbadon
On grounds of rounds of biers.

Here areology belies areas
Of casus belli with enallage,

As we, say, sigh
Sayonara and make up

Beds of acarpous red
Regolith read for unsigned

Life, trifles less
Lessons in cecity than surceases

In gests of just marginals,
The extant extent of acts

Worthy of thy iteration
To harp on the obviated vile

Vial of Dis tilled
Til told and dun

Paid, o penned sesame
Oped for Sterope strophe

On Oenomaus' lost race
As one minus us.

Fin Hoarse Meres

In the turd world the forth
e-States the filth column
Wheeled on *sesto senso*　　　　　　　戦争
 Toward seventh level eleve 'n

Heaved at octavo rima jobs,
The nth in decades that cascade
In decrescendo accounts *du jours*
And joules tongued in check

By jowly od souls
Who'd dun id to dearth
Under *sturm* un-ranked wrung
For the lasted numbers felt

Therein, the sicced muse
Of thus peers s-pied
At curved hohlraum rounded
On its elf for fended ends.

This why out, pleas
Note with standing what're
Insufficient funs, one less
You can torque ur-way

Out of dis on a hoarse
Mere with no gnome nym
Served wit less lessons
In pronoun striations of cased

Sheols *et quatours pour la fin
Du temps*, aka Pater and the fave
Fauves, the lost resort
Of journal ease outed

For walks on messianic wanters
The halve nuts knock,
The pow-wows that be in the burnt
Bush the lingo slung

At dogged gones on the raver
Nihil, wrong since sensed
As hour countdown done
And seconds chimera cum⌐.

The boilered prate of the times
Tombs the demotic in demonic
Collusions with bunkum mites
That might be zapped with apt

Jazz, a trip to the cento   先頭と銭湯
For macaronics and cheesy quips,
Hysteron proterons for bouleversement
Flaneurs on rai razzias

For the hypallage of the age, a biblio
Forking clasm in shaitan
Tmesis in ardor of afreet
For freedom from dumb flummery.

Come hear, rid all
That abut it, the news that stays
Mews and augers the Augean
Unstabled on lo-cal channels,

The sound of soi-disant chunder,
A quest to maxim-ize profits,
Infotainment antennae accost
With canny wariness else awls

Also lost, augeries with squib
Ankhs our auspices before hospices,
Rast breasted ope
Of diagonal gnosis as this,

Loc. cit., locks it,
A mutter of heuristic hym,
Through alas darks awkly
Until a nous worn lightly.

Repeat

It is perhaps, in no little degree, however, our propensity for the continuous – for the analogical – in the present case more particularly for the symmetrical which has been leading us astray. And, in fact, the sense of the symmetrical is an instinct which may be depended upon with an almost blindfold reliance. It is the poetical essence of the Universe – *of the Universe* which, in the supremeness of its symmetry, is but the most sublime of poems. Now symmetry and consistency are convertible terms: – thus Poetry and Truth are one. A thing is consistent in the ratio of its truth – true in the ratio of its consistency. *A perfect consistency, I repeat, can be nothing but an absolute truth.* We may take it for granted, then, that Man cannot long or widely err, if he suffer himself to be guided by his poetical, which I have maintained to be his truthful, in being his symmetrical, instinct. He must have a care, however, lest, in pursuing too heedlessly the superficial symmetry of forms and motions, he leave out of sight the really essential symmetry of the principles which determine and control them.

I repeat then – Let us endeavor to comprehend that the final globe of globes will instantaneously disappear, and that God will remain all in all

But are we here to pause? Not so. On the Universal agglomeration and dissolution, we can readily conceive that a new and perhaps totally different series of conditions may ensue – another creation and irradiation, returning into itself – another action and reaction of the Divine Will. Guiding our imaginations by that omniprevalent law of laws, the law of *periodicity, are we not, indeed, more than justified in entertaining a belief – let us say, rather, in indulging a hope – that the processes we have here ventured to contemplate will be renewed forever, and forever, and forever, a novel Universe swelling into existence, and then subsiding into nothingness, at every throb of the Heart Divine?*

And now – this Heart Divine – what is it? It is our own.

Let not the merely seeming irreverence of this idea frighten out souls from that cool exercise of consciousness – from that deep tranquility of self-inspection – through which alone we can hope to attain the presence of this, the most sublime of truths, and look it leisurely in the face.

The phaenomena on which our conclusions must at this point depend are merely spiritual shadows, but not the less thoroughly substantial.

-E. A. P., Eureka: A Prose Poem

In the symmetry of circular ratiocination,
Elliptical electric leakage

Moves metaphor for metaphor
Until P rim and rhyme

Orange and O range,
Find in spirit home.

I pass P on
And hearken crystallized O.

Reap EAP, repeat,
Excrete and create x,

Παρμενίδης ὁ Ἐλεάτης
not Eliotic

Nihilo nihil fit
P a line and o

The letter the law, o try
Poe as verse reverses

And I P slashes,
Face no po-faced

Po, ope the current
O elf selves, sprites and jets,

Red and blue halo
Trolls read as whiz

Kiddings levined. Should I
Piece my cued ps

Ad rem a dream and ream
Streams o vulgar fulgor

Runed in ruin nouned
Unknown, owned as O

P takes and ought
And not replete, should I

P myself off,
Lightening the rod to a comma

Comment anent event
Horizons, zones for periods

As radius vectors die
Laughing at the nous of the hang,

Mon? O woe   ᴾᑫ
Is wee if we weewee

All o tropes the way home
Rhymes and note not

Slants, o right, /   ॐ *my Emily*
Nitency in golden showers,

Telluric currents shown
In faculae, acoustical conductors,

Никола Тесла

O Schumann resonances, those longed
For ELF waves that *om*

ॐ

In at 7.83 Hz.
It hurts to hear actinism,

O coruscation o corruption, and nought
Know as loose vowels

Consonant with conned boggle
Mind finds infinitely

Open, your in out
To fluent ens, end

Means of meanings that intervene
Screens between streams

O causal nexi because other
Ether either matter

At atramentous absense, else
Wise wis were viz,

Scene for ceraunosocopy, o *coup
De foudre,* seen in second

Sight, no *animula vagula
Blandula* but veritable vajra,

वज्र

Chance to mind peise
In queued comets, discharge

Spontaneous combustion in airs
Right behind your ears:

Here's where the there's
Prose proceeds to try poet.

Poetrying

Ear Illyria, hear
Where Harmonia moaned after alpha-

Bet on bed of said
Round more sound than sense,

Lauds aloud, in engine
Gone on song, for sun

Of son, face of race
Amiss, elsewise, all ills,

The piths of myths missed
In irony, pyrite oneira,

Aureate arias art-
Lessly less than leese

Requires: quires that place
Names where air belongs,

Lays that blame by balm
The shame of lame claims

Of the human hum as some sum
Of summits, plummets dimitted

Of wit with its immitted admission,
Self ensorcelled from the source

Absent entia sent up
In opuses whose plusses use

Us as canorous scapes
In apes of shrape shaped

As country of tongue sprung
In swung counted tries,

Or *what you will* will
Tell in deed dead

In delivery, verily vacuous
Sans the *zhi-zhi* of trees

Aclick with crickets, the *za-za*
Of water asplash from a meter,

Absurd as surd unheard
In all of Sordello as Browning

Heedfully said from the head,   *Who will, may hear Sordello's story told*
The story's glory in inventory

Still awaiting the thrill
Of trill, poetrying being reading

Leading from seed to said,
The red thread made   紅線

Up of stirred stirrup,
Undull undulars attended.

Or you'd end in tapinosis,
No nose for gnosis, nous

Used to trace tacenda,
A tabellion who'd unbell the leonine

Nine and find the divine
Afflatus late, laid

In aphony, dumbed and downed
In the offing, our species' specialty,

Copy cacoepy, open
Cecity, cease as raucity

Reaches each indifferent
Ear in different rents

Unto nullibiety, nill alibi,
Lair of Lear after all's

Said undone, until *the rain*
It raineth every day,   *Cf. Feste*

The end of repetends utter
Error trued to madness

Made in idiot idiom
To come to comedy as zombie,

Listless listening in last
Throes thrown no throne,

No analogy in angelology, no lodge,
Ledge, dodge, edge,

Or od, poetrying tried
And unfound, sound confounded?

How to Read a Poem

Keep your crass eyes crossed
And your tease dotty, doughty

Ties to try poetry
At its limits, its limens limns

O Os as it were that wear
And tear tarantism from *to*s

Tipped as psithurism rhythms
And tide brontide rides

To petrichor poured chords
That lodge lethologica in comical

Chronicles o periodical calls
In beats nicked sic,

So feet synthesize synesthesia,
A trick saintly Trichosanthes

Sends out in petals that tell
The noughts o night how light

Reaches speech in each
Trigger figure o fugue

O brogue broken to parole
Soul in sound holes

You hear to there where air
Abides in abderian dares

Past agelasts for ages lasted
By philological *lo*s lowed

Till beheld in words as deeds
Heeded and headed om.

Loaded Words

To prime time for decline
And fall (the umbrella the retinue

Held over the daimyo as he went
In procession when summoned to face

The god called emperor became
A spike, *sandai gasa*),   参内傘

Humbled don down
And done to dumb dun,

Cf. scilla as squilla as Scylla
After sicced by lovesick Circe,

For as any fabled name   大名
Should know there's no lord

Of war, all warlords
In precession of equinoctial knocks

Block and lock heads,
All words loaded

And laded unto late *un*   運
Until history is story shored

To share in fair game
That moves with behoofed *têtes*

A *téter* world records,
Genji the gonzo journal

Of the day, or the say of Shakespeare
On the *mali belli* of the Roses,

Roads that lead to lead
Unless led to Logos,

The lego form to corner
Stones and take stains

Of sacrifice that suffice to suffer
Us to come through scathed,

Saved alone by self-
Solfege from bare airs,

Ready to declare a theatre
Of conjurations by every other

Noun known and verbed
Would creep to crepe, murder

For Myrtle until we're martyrs,
Mortal morals mere

Matter to mutter minus
Mothered wit for art's

Part, sake of purple
Passages to hum and hymn

Us unto our makers, markers
Of time that tide us up,

Over and out, of breath
The very inspiration varied

To take the blow and bow
Out grace until we stay

The flow to florescences of no
Sense, scent or tint

Other than ones that wander
In wonder to amuse a muse

To music what were otherwise
Amaranth, to math metrics

To menses of manses of man
And the guerdon of a garden of darned

And loomed lunes that dam
Our damnation as long as song

Sings the fringes that singe
In sensation to sensational sense,

That convergence of sins in aesthesia
That ethers the ethereal to anthems

On anthers sans answers which question
Quests to taste tests

In texts the rectos of wrecks
Versos reverse in verses,

Else better to lie
Nameless and blameless in less

Conscious nests next
To unmulled nulls full

Of things that sting and sing
Not; nought blows

On leas as leaseless as these
Leaves with griffonage left

To apes to ape japes,
Trace numbers and numerals

To minerals, carbon absent
Car to *mot* or *bon*

Bones, all *mals*
Du fleur blurs that err

On mum emmeleia and summed
Unsoundness of propellers of prepollence.

No Such Agency

O huma, home o *om*
O peri, less periplus than periergy

O this that ne'er alights
O'er lights and flickers o phoenix

O fornix for musics o tuba
Tree and absentee scree

O Koh Talism o Tin
Man in land o strand

O unseen sea, scene
Gleaned from sheen o screened

Dream deemed ream
O rim o rhyme, prime

Unnumb numbers o hum
As sun o wonderments met

In wanders where air carries
Sound sound to resound

Zetetic tacks o texts
In perscrutation o notation o nought

Not netted in reflexions o x,
As Cyanopica cyanus signs us

Through through and through throes
O mock mockery o talk

Ticked off on sick sics
O senses sans sense o ens

As ending beginning to sing
A mystic mist take,

Ache after a long flight
O stares at far stars,

Harkening arks to know
With no such agency,

If not adjacency o cadency o oneiromancy,
Fancy to see secrets

As settings o sums spun
To puns pumped through pampas

Glassed as if if lifted
Drafts after larks after darks

Righted by indited indicted
Climate calamity in climb

O momentous moment, meant
Mentia, dimension o mention

O O zone, phone
Blown to atone flown

Aesthesia, seize Shiva
And own parousia in pursuance.

Slow Light

Horology o horror o orrery
O error o escapement meant

As mechanism for talk's tics
Away from the ruth o truth,

Forsooth the torque o known *non,*
Like trick o tourbillon on quantum

O gravity o no knowing,
Sings o signs o silence

O sloe hole, slower
O C to unseen scene

O circle squared to no O,
Horrisonous horizon, zone

O prolepsis o lapse, collapse
O all calls, fall

O time past rhyme, last
Grasp gasp as asp

Clasps and offs blasts
To dumbed numb numbers

In final finale, lay
O O sans olé to say

Prescience, no science save o the never
Saved or obviated obvious,

Is sense sent sensibility,
Sensitivity o nativity as itty,

Bit o bite o blight,
Time times O;

So songs long,
Long since, for gong o wrong

To wring to ring a ring
Around in rounds o sounds o O.

Heart o Art

The heart hath no relief but breaking
-Thomas Moore, *Lalla Rookh*

From functions sheaves, curves
O branes, as automorphic forms

Know *om* in harmolodics,
Leave reeves and ring

Langlands from unseen sea,
Realm that whelms real,

Where sick siiankos cause
Unhallowed hollows and bellows

Below loud bows o tall
Talipot trees that seize

And freeze leese in friezes,
As the kerna cornet nets

Deafened defenders who find
Nycanthe in the cant o can't,   *those hellish fires that light*
                                   The mandrake's charnel leaves at night

Moored by samoors, more
Lessened than *les âmes damnées,*

Those Thracian thrashers that flat-hat
Ceaselessly, unless Israfil is,

Retrilled till the time at the tone
O the Tonquin goldfinch clinches

The haunts of the fount found
In Chindara wherein love laves

And leaves as Camadeva, comes
With the scent o the Nagacesara sans caesura,

As Amrita rite, writ   अमृत
O the tree o the tomb o Tan-Sein,

Jumbo jambul with bulbul
Eggs, yggdrasil abysmal,

As is this, if theses o la-la
Rooks rock your talk

With ticks o the heart o art,
The light o the haram that rights

Barren signs it sings, and O
If there be an Elysium on earth

    It is this,
    It is this.

Un

Felix nihil admirari
        -Horace, Epistles I, vi, 1

What the music I love
expresses to me is not thought
too <u>*indefinite*</u> *to be put into words,*
but, on the contrary, too <u>*definite*</u>.
-Felix Mendelssohn, letter to Marc-André Souchay, 15 October 1842

The forces that force us, fierce
Facets o the obviously oblivious,

Obviate nought not known
O others authored into either ether

Or orthodox docks o dotty
Gaia scienza senza sense

O *syne* as sign o episteme
Teeming dicament o mentis,

As is meant, with so long
Songs o twinges singed

O passing passion shunning
Careless caresses for essences

O melancholy calling all jolly
Follies o moly gall

O amphiboly, fibs o melopoeia,
Poe facing the aching

Phases o phrases in blazons
O para-Dis, this dell

O Bel fell knell,
Spell o expelled misses,

Meta met in metrics,
Eureka!, tricks o the quick

Fore the farces o dark
Unharkened slippages o ages

Argue argute routes
O canny argybargy till cant

Levers lovers to leftovers
O exposures as posers o throes

No thrones pwn, only puns
Open in O zones

As sounded stounds stood,
Ods even as bollixes call

Felicities in cited cecities
As aspirations suspire in pyre

Rite writ o paronyms, 一
Saw the they, moan

物の哀れ

O no awa ray, zen
Zooked, do caw, 一   दुःख

As Par'o no Mas see
ə, uh-uh, until a mused

Bemusement o *un* tell   運
O ells one here ear

To bear the uncared for there,
The air where 'El dwell.   אֵל

Wots in a Paronym?

By homely
gifts and
hindered Words the human
heart is told of nothing —
'Nothing' is
the force that renovates
the World —

-Emily to Susan Dickinson, *Letters* 1958, L1563

Hyper, I come to hypericum,
Wort o wort o sort

O said thread read,
Yet fret at threat met

Enveloped as in the belle's cell's
Calls to all as un—

Dashed ashes o unabashed
Amor more adored in dared

Blancs and blinks than in inked
Links to guised sighs

Sized as seizures see
Sawn *it*s in minute

Tinges o contingency, tangs
O pangs o *tangere* o *noli*

Me, the me o my sign singed
Signifier o smoke and mere

Mare's tale o stalled
Nacht o nocht nought

Who's there as rare air
Squared to numen o pneuma

O sound round O,
Flower o our lo flow.

Scotography

The chert chart o art,
The gabbro o gab lab,

The meta for or o metaphor,
Ores for selling solid

Airs, point to painted pains
Taking tricks to torque

Tics that sic sic
Musics o our msecs to parsec

Cant levers o leaves
And line repined signs

As math to paths o Jagganath
That map salmon maps

O *eaux* to see these theses
As we wee weirds word

Our way to say how stars
Start and startle still

The gaze phase till phrase
Faze our teased yet tased

Sense since sediment o sentiment
To meant mettle o M

As measure o the may o sure
Be bent light righted

In written tensions as shunned
Shunts, stunts past stunted

Lasts as *un*s pun   運
Pens unto ens in outed

Routes o roots routed
By byes to eyed seeds,

Scenes o gleaned screens
O Gaia via maya.

Quadrate Probe

The precuneus, canniest crux
O flux o axon offices

Offing disservice to deserve
Desserts and desert deserts

O dearths o arts, prenucleus
O new muses, uses

Susses o plexuses to express
Impressions o misprisions o passions

As actions like try-ons eye
High *lo*s o *O*s,

As elect sections o *x*es
Noun unknowns to cue

Nous plus *lux* in flux,
As annular lunar tunes

Shade blood to brew
Brooding on blues trued

In calls o melancholy, the melopoeia
O Poe facing the erasure

O surety, purity and pretty
Much Mach one mocking

Making as taking faking
To subprime minus sublime, short

Giraffe graphs o gravitational
Lensing, (sic) xeric gaze

O insomnia contra chimera
As oneiric as entheogenic, for psychonautic

Nods to od for awed
Lauds o laws o escalades

To climb to climes like lilac
Delights as pilots o violet

Twilight ligate to migrate
With windborne Swinburne, turn

Churn o yearning to learning
And fear to sphere o sheer

Vigilance, chance for dance
To embody bodhi and bode

Lodes o odes, nodes
O goads past encoded loads

O no knowing till telling —
(Hell to ells o elephant

Hierophants who'd hoot and *chant*
Du cygne as sign o surds,

Mere fantasias o phrases sans seity,
Haecceity o city o cecity,

Telemetry o prosody o apostrophes,
Prophecy o porism o perorations,

Alveromancy o chances o cancer,
Predated predator o cells

As bells told to hold
Sound unsound, drones

For those in throes o prose)
— goes for epiphany in polyphony,

Opening unto moly o *om*
As Hermes homes terms

O oscine singing to scene
O song prolonged in gleaning

Sheen from screen, mean
O meaning o O o all.

Hyades to Hades

But the Quincunx of Heaven runs low,
and 'tis time to close the five ports of knowledge.
-Thomas Browne, The Garden of Cyrus

Rex rode his oryx
To Styx, where he stopped at ped-
Xing and petted
His petulant pet then mis-
Read exit and crossed to X.

Aye, 'tis time for a Blake
Dance with the ghost o a rose,

In ∞ without an umpire,   *roll x*
Senseless, sans empire, pyre

O heliacal rising in simile
O Semele, seme o orange

O o October over O_2
Rhymed to cometical coma,

Comedy o Chronos that lows
Noesis is not just note

O night, it hights history
As is is story o hysteresis,

Hysterical call o fall
And laughter after all palls

And light plights troth
With Thoth, author o othered

Threads read in red
Shifts as *ifs* o life

Left to nexus o plexus
O *X*s expended in extended

Obumbration, as occultation and osculation
School skews to clues

O muses true in losing,
Singing excruciate signings,

Crosses o cosmic palindromes,
Drones o *N* known

In acts o actinic nitency
As asterism rhythms Rhadamanthus

To *pass the ferry backward,*   *Areopagitica*
Glass the airy wrack word,

Chasse the Feri wakeboard,
Torque *the orc o a close.*

      Cotillon o yon
      Yin x yang, O², le monde
      O moaned om homed in
      Allemande left righted to
      Write Hyades to Hades.

117

祝詞 [1]

This impasto o the past is patible
In glassed vasts o crafts

Asked after arts' parts
Chart the smarts o the heart

To divine the chine o the line
In signs o benign design,

As exponents o exponential entia,
As tics o the ilk o silk

Filaments inform the maker
Like fakir quivers, deliver

Qui vive viva voce, the swerve
To serve verb as verve,

Mere mirror no more,
Nor ether o other there,

Rather the air paired with dares
O here heard o surds,

*because not to know
something is a complicated
process which takes place
beneath the shadow of the truth*
-Krasznahorkai, *Seiobo There Below*

As *music is the gloom o one*
عمر بن علي بن الفارض
Disowned o the om o home,

豆 whom doom yet rooms
In moans o *un* owned,

運

*these decorations aren't even
decorations but the infinities*
Toned and tuned ruins
of a language
Trued in toons as lunar
-Krasznahorkai, *Seiobo There Below*

*it is certain that this
origin is as unclear*

118

Albedo bids a boded
Beat to embed dread

And read shifts o ifs
O *x*s to exstasis as basis

O known Os, as *lo*s
Low lies to laws

That awe, ods odds
Kin o keen een

E'en when yen for meant
Mounts outed means

O meaningless lessons o songs
Sans sense o essence o since,

Time's rhyme with numbers
Unnumb to primes minus

Us, the hush o dust
Lays allay as alae

O angels signal entanglement,
Extravagant abandon donned.

as the origin of any
work of art can be
-Krasznahorkai, Seibo There Below

---

1. Norito, or, as writ by László Krasznahorkai, in Seiobo There Below, via Ottilie Mulzet, "the belief that the uttered word has power, but only the word uttered correctly, faultlessly, beautifully has the power to bring good; every time the opposite occurs, the word will instead signify something bad for the community." Cf. 言霊, kotodama, the Japanese belief that mystical powers dwell in words and names. English translations include "soul of language," "spirit of language," "power of language," "power word," "magic word," and "sacred sound". The notion of kotodama presupposes that sounds can magically affect objects, and that ritual word usages can influence our environment, body, mind, and soul.

Auscult

Dubbing yarn is slub
As dumbing amoebaeum is sub-

Obtuse ossuary o sound
Sense minded o ground

Base, case o betrayed
Traces o *ars* arrayed

Unparsed in forces o farces
O harkenedness, *parque* carcasses

Newsed as mews amuses,
Bouches boshed sans recuses,

Parodes as eroded as monodies,   *O Meí!*
Melodies melded in threnodies

As doozy don'ts wont
To too truthiness *sont*

Sons tous trémoussants,
Éloignment moins doucement,

Quelle langue gone on wrong
Gangue, gonged song

Mered to pong, *merde*
Made o air bared

In dystory as destiny o tinny
Ear, ninny whinny

Here as jinni jeers
In doggerel that growls and disappears

Instead o steadying in studying
Howlers and stubborn muddying

As traducements, inducements to muse
Sicced to skinny that trues

As blues lose delusions
To loose disillusions sans conclusions,

So auscult occulted calls
And culls, catch what falls

Away in galling surdity
Or bawls all as turd ditty,

This ink included unblinked,
No purview pure o tinct,

Else pixels lated by emoji
Shows, O closed shoji,

O no-see cars far from heard
As ghastly ghost words slurred.

Hygiantics:
Musicology and Philology[1]

De Phylide

Aurea sidereos cum forte reduceret ignes
　　Prospiciens dulci lumine cuncta Venus,
Efferri fato cum sensit Phyllida acerbo
　　Functam, et pallenti fronde virere comas,
Parcere non lacrimis potuit, non ore querelis
　　His mestam duris se abstinuisse dea,
Militia, hem, re a nostra, et dulci a coniuge Phylli,
　　O decus innuptarum, abstulit atra dies.

　　'Εκ τῶν τῆς Σοφοκλέους 'Αντιγόνης.
　　　　　τὰς γὰρ ἡδονὰς
　　ὅταν προδῶσιν ἄνδρες, οὐ τίθημ' ἐγὼ
　　ζῆν τοῦτον, ἀλλ' ἔμψυχον ἡγοῦμαι νεκρόν.

-Girolamo Mei[2]

Lo those lowering high
　　Notes no welkin wells
Nor elegy assuages, no swedge
　　In sedge as pale palls,
As breath death recks
　　In desinence sent to sonance
Mei measures in days[3]
　　As atramentous as anamnesis o anabasis;
In the keenness o Venus' cothurnus
　　No bourn o norn known
Spares airs from tares
　　Or tears for sheared weirds,　　　　　*vox et praeterea nihil*
Documents debouched to nullibiety,
　　All pasigraphy past lasts,
The fits o fyttes fates,
　　Entries o antre o *Angelus*　　　　　*behold Benjamin*
Novus, no orifice redivivus,　　　　　*pace Plato*
　　Save *aux abois, à bas*
Humbug o defunct tongues,

Adjunct steganography spelunked
Scant ken canted,
Shades played out in clades,
Renderings tendered sans surrendering
As the end (no *and* at hand)
Falls, *semper Phylli,* o lied.

1. Cf. Donatella Restani, L'Itinerario di Girolamo Mei dalla "Poetica" alla Musica, Firenze: Olschki, 1990, 61: "La storia della recezione del locus platonico da parte filologi, analogamente a quella relative al testo di scuola peripatetica emendato nel De modis, conferma la plausibilità delle ipotesi e soprattutto la validità dell'impostazione metodologica di Mei. Si potrebbe rimodellare, pertanto, una celebre pointe, sotolineando, con un sorriso, che Mei tentò per una volta, almendo, di mutare quella 'zitella arcigna' inamorata di Apollo, che è Musicologia, per mezzo di un'amicizia vera con la 'amorosa e amabile' Filologia."

2. See Restani, 96: "Dal buio nel quale ancora oggi sono immerse alcune opera attribuite a Mei dale coeve biografie fiorentine manoscritte, e di cui le lettere recano trace, elencanti, tra le altre, quattro tragedie e un libro di sonnetti, è ritornata alla luce una sola elegia Latina." The lines from Sophocles' Antigone may be rendered: "Now all is gone. For when a man has lost what gives him pleasure, I don't include him among the living — he's a breathing corpse."

3. Cf. Restani, 11: "Mei avocava a sé solamente l'occupazione intellettuale, esprimendo il 'nuovo' senso di disagio per la profonda rapport committente-letterato, propria dell'ultimo Cinquencento."

Aqua Vitae

Mais je crie et mon cri me vaut tant de coups sourds
Qu'assommé crâne en feu tombé je beugle et mords
Et dans l'effondrement des sous-sols des racines
Tout au fond des entrailles de la terre et du ventre
Je me dresse à l'envers le sang solidifié
Et les nerfs tricoteurs crispés jusqu'à la transe
Piétinez piétinez ce corps qui se refuse
A vivre au contact des morts
Que vous êtes pourris vivants cerveaux d'ordures
Regardez-moi je monte au-dessous des tombeaux
Jusqu'au sommet central de l'intérieur de tout
Et je ris du grand rire en trou noir de la mort
Au tonnerre du rire de la rage des mort
    -Roger Gilbert-Lecomte, *"Le fils de l'os parle"*

This cirrus script trips
Spirit despite ecthlipsis

O *M* from *om* when *O*
Owes *eau* to ether,

And Tellus mars Mars,
As told us in bound domain   *This That*

Theory to ear as or
Either there or here,

As strings ring zings
O monstrous moonshine to Circean

Seizure sirened in Byron-
Like lacks to equivoques

O vogue vagaries, aqua
O Acheron fossae, face

124

O recurring slope linae,
Life rife with rivens,

Untied ifs and raven-
Ings winged in Gs

Strung in waited lessness,
Mass o marooned neutrino,

No knowing through episteme semes,
Sums o O squared to ne'er, $\sigma_x \sigma_p \geq \frac{\hbar}{2}$

The agiotage o language alienage,
The shelf o self, reference

Sentenced to semblance, presence
O absence, aposiopesis parsed,

Last grasp passed,
Past glassed and asked,

As cluster amaryllis stamens
Listen or SETI sites eye

Red threads read   赤い糸
Till time rimes with airs

Primed and fair fares
Strive for archived lives

Guarded by retarded bards
O lost causes, glosses

The cost o our hours o dross
To suss *l'os* from loss,

Âme from *amen, I am*
Before יהוה was,

Divine verve in swerve
To verse Os in recked OHs。

Elected Affinities

As Goethe gets gimleted
By Benjamin, meaning screening

To osmose operose opus,
So Magritte greets secrets

O the part o parthenogenesis in art,
As Oneiroi alloy ploys

That cloy and annoy to joy,
As alchemy o academy in polysemy,

O echoes o Eco, o the affinity
O lists to list toward infinity,

The home o *om* known
In monody since Mei made way

To say (*mes amis, écoutez
L'histoire*), from grimoire to *gloire*,

Adam as quondam damn
To give and forgive as factitive

Figures are apertures to overtures,
Or arias airs for heirs

Owned down to to ground
Bass, — the base o the grace

To poetry Poe po-
Faced sufficed till the spliced

Hex o the hoaxes yoked
"The Bells" to hell's ells,

Reading leading to heeding
Porosity or lost glasnosts,

Frenemies the ends that amend,
Invite us to recite or blight

Stuff, — o rough writers
Et alia o the aboulia o alalia,

Palilalia, echolalia, or glossolalia
In lays that bray sans play

O friendship, the trip that ends
Nought as an f-stop op

Opens pens to the O
O our part athwart swart

Times in rhymes that prime
The mind twined to blind

Amor that glamours grammar
Till cecity cease in Greece

As metaphor for store o score
O *modis musicis,* as is

This dative native to creative
Electives as stimulative iteratives,

Recursions o versions o verse
Re: selves salved if not saved,

Those chosen that disclose the Os
O our hours as powers to peruse.

Air de cours

Scriabin's psilocybin descried
In mystic mist misses

Concordances o chords as dances
O harmolodic ods in periods

O aesthesia that see beyond Sym
In om homed in moans

O monodies with the odd oud
Or theorbo for orbs o verbs

Re: nouned sounds in sonnet
CXXVII — see exes vie

For kisses — ad Kalendas called
Graecas — Eroicas that destroy

Hand spans, transcendence   *Réminiscences de Don Juan*
Sans sense mensed, whence ens

Ends in fathoms o Antiphons —
O phones o tone tone

Zones, o Zoist list
O metas physicked in music

As phasic arousal — O ouzel —
Is versal, reversal o SAL,

O soul as droll toll,
Tholed hole, no goal

Save in clave as phrasing
Referent, afferent o rent

On *on* blown by bones,   音
As by Byron, non-Oberon or Arawn,   *The Vision of Judgement*

Anatman the etymon o John,
The weird o the word heard,   अनात्मन्

So soterial trial, all
O pleroma as soma, is sum   аккорд плеромы

O songs, from sombre chats
To schlegels, angels o plagals,

Amen to *Mysterium,* delirium
Come from ciborium to auditorium.   *Pyx specs*

Linear Near

The eye of man hath not heard,
the ear of man hath not seen
-Shakespeare, *A Midsummer Night's Dream*

Agonic agon gone
Spawns non-conned pawn

O cant yet can scan
Pans to fan vans

Wrung by lungs to rungs
Strung as runs for tongues

To savor, favor o savers
O raves laved in waivers

O sense yet tense with mense
O dense portents, hence

Dolor o rale toll
Till goal o soul's role

Rhymes I'm with mime
Primed for climb to chime

Sound rounded to redound,
The confounded bound to the profound

In linear near, here
Queer seer ear

O ne'er, bare air
Clair, dare fare.

Sum

Do the Math 101

Donner un sens plus pur aux mots de la tribu
Proclamèrent très haut le sortilege bu
  -Stéphane Mallarmé, "Le Tombeau d'Edgar Poe"

You do you. Do
The math. Be all you

Can be. I did it
My way. It's literally a zero-

Sum game. The bottom line
Is it's not rocket

Science. It all adds
Up. It boils down

To a brain drain on a bad
Hair day. No, it's a no-

Brainer, I can't even.
You read my mind. It

Fell through the cracks, with the game
On the line. It's on the tip of my tongue,

To pay lip service to the path
Of least resistance. To push

The envelope, save your breath.
Get a second opinion and count

Your blessings. When all is said
And done, you can say that

Again. Not to repeat myself,
But I couldn't get a word in

Edgewise. So get with the program.
We're on the same page, but you're

Not playing with a full deck.
So why not take all of me?

Are you putting me on? The proof
Is in the pudding, it says here.

No pun intended, even
As we speak. There's no rhyme

Or reason to it. Game over,
At the end of the day. To sum up,

Life is hard, and then you
Die. Get over it. It's

A dream come true. Now
You're talking. Just put two

And two together to do due
Diligence. Less is more.

Do as I say, not as I
Do. No way. I'm

An open book. Which part
Of do don't you understand?

A Decade o Roundels

i

Tree o Glee

As round o roundel sounds the bounds o bourn
O song, so air is singing its *qi* in key   ⌐
O seeing beyond the cecity of o the sites o the born
    From tree o glee.

As a circle squared to dare a sea o free
Verse to rehearse a reverse into an *O* not lorn,
So Norn are known in blown tones o nebulae.

As radicles call till Yggdrasil fills the morn
O mourning and night o blight with sigil o three
Degrees, so Πάν ποιεῖν puns alien horn
    From tree o glee.

ii
Hark in the Dark

See saw-whet seize breeze from tree
Or hear how owl ear allow bough
To serve verve as berth for 3D
    Seeking in cecity.

For death in dearth to breathe by, bequeath a tao
For sound sounding in Cimmerian chimera to bee
气 E'en wee *qi,* as *xi* allow, and how   悉 *(know)*

Læs sough in locating Skelton key
For quicklime rimes in lines rounded to scrow
Descried as lies o lays, as plays o *esprit*
    Seeking in cecity.

iii

Hu

Ondine is to *ondo* as soul to Coelus, locus   音頭
O Orcus course as orchestra o tantra tantara,
Lo *tous songes sont mensonges,* focus
        O *eau* and air.

As songs long for currawong cures for samsara,
Rhythms to rhyme as catechisms o cataclysms o Cocus

Κοϊοσ?   Question quests, so ken is kith o kithara.

The hum o human is to *hu* o M as hocus   हु
O O is to trow o known *n* in sayonara,
So music is mesic, means o crocus and Phocus,
        O *eau* and air.

iv

Out of blue into black is the scheme of the skies

Nimbi be limbi o *eau* and air, *ambiances*
As dances o entranced transience, as sciences o nescience,
Vapors o paper in books cooked to assonances
    O nebulous nous.

Loud clouds be utter matter, too intrinse
To unloose, though on off rhymes the sounds o *alliances*
Count quanta to round roundels to prescience,

As *Nephelidia* be lied to light benighted adamances
O surdity to quiddities o jubilated obnubilated ambisenses,
Strands to stand the helices o hell, od audiences
    O nebulous nous.

v

ᚠᛏᛗ

As a supermoon looms, croon a lunatic tune,
Sing pericynthion syntheses o Semele similes,
Stimula simulars, and Diana anas, rune
     Alu to true voodoo.

Ride the tides o lieder to read seas
And seize *Os* as flows to know by swoon,
To come around to sound and see by reprise

O *om*, an alveromancy to home poem to hewn
Nous o use o spheres o music as keys
To perceive the singing o things, to commune and attune
     Alu to true voodoo.

vi

for Evan Parker

Magic is tragic — *lo Prospero* — and prospects o woe
Make miracles *clefs* o makers, romances as dances
Move air as bodes o bodies and phonemes low
      Obsolete *od* to deeds.

The lord o words teaches tautologies as chances
For λογος to lodge with droll ells o flow
O *prana* as ana o circular calls o trances   प्राण

After laughter and flutter o utterance out to go
On on *O* as tracks o sax in manses
O fancy, primary seconds o *on* that blow   音
      Obsolete *od* to deeds.

vii

Reap repeats as deeps to deed to heart
As metaphor for parts that strap arts to stars
And mirror airs to ears in chants that impart
    The cause and *mos* o cosmos.

Performance perforce deforms, our powers cars
O far fractomancy and close facticity to chart
Tâtonnement o tones and atone for grimoires in *glories*

O assays that essay said head and depart
On constant constraints unto haint haunts o ares
As bizarres athwart *errare,* starts to art
    The cause and *mos* o cosmos.

viii

Entanglement angles alien angels home,
Ideality ties to try with photosynthetic fits
O *lieder* lit to emication as skiagraphy o tome
      O hypnotic knots o nought,

While life midwifes trials o wits then quits,
Its tragic acts o gods begot a syndrome
O throes o woes in bondage to age as flits

O time as rhyme o nebulae nullibiety, no gloam,
Space a race o energy to anergy, a blitz
O obliteration, the fate o the known a gnome
      O hypnotic knots o nought.

ix
for Ornette Coleman

The blues true our hours o rue to purview
O our power to scour our weird with eared
Eyes and size the sighs that imbue adieu
    With due delves o selves

As abysms ride rhythms that writhe with sphered
Light and write the night in nitency to construe
Déjà vu muses in hues that hear the disappeared

And queered o od in harmolodic rhapsodies that cue
Q values that eschew Pandemonium moans with cleared
Acuity o the contiguity o universe in us to pursue
    With due delves o selves.

X
for Jerome McGann

As ψυχομαχία with maker, experiment meant as Περὶ
ὕψους suss o Panic dust, the scholar's
Art parts the seizures o soundings to carry
　　　X across to hypertext.

As the tensions o the perplexities o "The Bells" for callers
Tell the future o literature, no stationary aerie
O airs or hell o roundels sans sense for scrawlers

O squalors in lores o smeared ears, here dare nary
As O o known unknowns to own as Mahler's
Allures cure excruciates in polyphony and ferry
　　　X across to hypertexts.

Calculus

As exigent exit is X,
The algebra o gibbered burr,

Urge to scream and scram
Crammed with crambo o dammed

Damns, the n o ens
Ended in dead letters,

Lalochezia ceasing to serve
Verve, oeuvre swerved

To complaints slain by aints,
No known owned

Or imagined, magi mad
Delusions sans stars as horrisonous

Horizons eventuate late
Light, caliginous nous,

Through Theia see thee,
Selene, in isotopes o O,

Trow the blow that bestows,
The flow aglow in throes

O *lo*s in loss, as loess
Leeses yet leases pieces

In surceases that seize keys
To see in low albedo,

As alcedo cede in *eaux*
The X o life rife

In vised Ys, whys
That answer after wise laughter

That lunacy in euphony is cosmogony,
The gone come Om,

Reposed in prosopopoeia, that calculus
As calls cull us

Plus α bets on odds
O od as god o escalades

To clamber to clamor chambers
O ground sound rounded

To prime numbers to hum
Some sum o undumb come.

Atomic Number One

As hydrangeas rain, so I
Absorb sounded lie,

The soiled acidic blues
Phantom limb rues

Lead to cul-de-sac
Bed where pink wrack

Recks shift in tone,
Dilation of eye, phone

Blown to quantum of loss
Nigh joss in gloss,

Glassed smoke of alibi
Nullibiety times gibi, (2^{30})

Gibberish summed to curtal
Couple to rime detrital,

PS pH number
Mense from numb to number.

The 4% Premonstration

The straight state O
The galactic tic, its

Warped bowl, saddle,
Or fedora, correlates with orbits

O Magellanic Clouds through, lo,
Haloes o dark matter,

Scattering a cosmic wake,
That smattering that γ ray

Bursts burst as constant
Handle on standard candles,

Our 4% sent
Out to the tremendous atramentous,

Those old novas dated
To light years right

Back to black force,
Enforcer o blank banks

O accounts o counts to continua,
Number and verse o universe

Where cinder stellas stalk
Red embers to bed,

Then rock clock to atomic
Nought, telltale told

To hold beholders down
To dumbed done and said.

Accretion Discs

As an antithesis to the Antikythera mechanism
Seek not the Cyclades cycle

Of concoction and iconoclasm; Keros
Cared not about gears or graphy

And rifted glyphs, but there too
Faced space and figured,

Conjured means to conjoin
Canny measures and the incomputable,

With folded arms fielded
Chimaeras foaled and failed;

No, not for millennia
Did imagination count to counters

For such wonderments of form and formulation,
Until artifice sufficed to surface

The countenances of the deep in none
One clutches, digits

Opened to the peril of the puerile,
The cult of cute, kitty

Hallowed in culture hollowed
Not to nought yet not

Ana to log Logos,
Legos, rather, that block knots

To nodes of od for odes,
Our orts motes from the got

Gone in the details dovetailed
With the deficits of disordered attention,

Hard driven to choose
Other than snooze news,

Worn soft headed
For more mirrored mores,

As images minus the ward
Of the word art not art,

Less sense, space
Dust signed by γ

Reports from unhorizoned events,
Cingular nooses sans loop

De loops, accretion discs
Which disperse past and parses

Until the told is you
Tubed and stoppered in snuffing

Films over acumen snorting
In asphyxia with soundless grammar

For ∞, Möbius chirality
Cythereans saw through,

Glasses to gloss and gliss
And O on and on in.

Grave Waves

for Keith A. Rose

From math polished to polymath
Paths o apotropaic craics,

From candle to Chandler and unrandom
Damn dumb numbers[1]

O holes in *dynamic multicolor*
Displays of the Fourier transform

Of the Euler Eta function,
And on to a *fortification problem*

With roses because our local
Deer consider them a delicacy

In spite of their thorns; for the first
Few years any such plant

Has to grow in a rather burly
Cage: this sage gauged

Fine lines and mined
Mind to divine signs,

O grave waves, brave
Enclaves o staved aves,

Ere eared valleys o *vales,*[2]
Event horizons as zones

O cecity as ceaseless loss,
No rose compass or bypass

O $G_{\mu\nu} = \frac{8\pi G_N}{c^4} T_{\mu\nu}$,
Though one done punned it:

O K. Rose arose on ridden
Rhythm, a room o one,

Owned as languaged by Lord Dunsany:
[Consult any dictionary, but in vain]

Like that ma'am in Amherst and unlike
"The Raven," for example [which] stands

Up just fine in any
Number of languages, as "The Mirror

Cracked" naturally quotes
The Lady of Shallot, the original

Of the fame of that line.
Since I was reading it

In Spanish, I naturally tried
To translate it back into English.

Couldn't remember the original
At all. The important thing

Is the life lesson in The Lady.
Don't go chasing after

Or mooning about handsome strangers.
If The Lady had stuck to her weaving,

She'd be weaving there still.
You could tell she was happy

As a clam what with the singing....
And the name of the poem which begins

"All in green went my
Love riding," which I love   or our Laura?

By the way, an example of the way
The internet spreads errors

Around. You will find the poem
All over the place with an obvious

Typo. O eros topos,
E'er erose, aired,

Another year struggling
To keep my rosebushes alive

In a resentful environment, like trying
To come to cummings in an alien

Tongue; no Portuguese nor Norwegian,
So Sven Elvestad, or any seven

Pen names, in penumbral *Walden-
Samkeit* till *Torschlusspanik* to Max

Schraut, shrouded out loud
Till *I'll figure it out*

Or they can write that I didn't
As my epitaph. Will try

Not to be such a (deleted)
During the coming year. **Ear**

Here clear gears,
Watch repaired nautch

O Ramanujan, no Unabomber: *you*
Can imagine what my cabin looks

Like, with all those antiques
Strewn around. Floor is in short

Supply. So ply the Voynich
Manuscript...still don't know

What language it's in. They call
It Voynichese; it's good with Gouda.

You eidetic types, no sympathy.
I wish you the Cream of the Jest,

Zest for slowly going
Through Don Quijote, it's a little

Hard since he talks
In pretty artificial prose.

I don't need to get
All the jokes anyway.

Remember the affair of the fuller's
Mills? The story of Childe

Roland and the Dark Tower
The only significant one

I know that traces back
To a nursery rhyme. You

Probably already know
The metrical model of Hiawatha.

The ruth truth o youth,
That slices o trice need suffice,

Led the lad to lay
Away a way to replay

Lost clauses as causes
O pause laws, courses

O curses o portal coils,
Oil toils, foiled

Orders o weird wiring,
Harnesses hight the highness

O the Triumph o darkness and the Parca
Carcasses o ragged Jags,

Engines o ginned ends,
Designed leaks, freak

Refractions, tricks o blight,
Acts o rations o facts,

Cracks o lax lacks
In thrall to the thalweg dregs

O semblances tranced to remembrances
O revenant ferries, his buoyage

Voyage to Arcturus, lo us Icaruses,
Or durous tsuris through thesauruses,

And I a mock theta
Function, no unction, just unjust

Reduction and redaction o fractions,

$$\int_0^\infty \frac{1 + x^2/(b+1)^2}{1 + x^2/(a)^2} \times \frac{1 + x^2/(b+2)^2}{1 + x^2/(a+1)^2} \times \cdots \; dx = \frac{\sqrt{\pi}}{2} \times \frac{\Gamma(a + \frac{1}{2})\Gamma(b+1)\Gamma(b-a+1)}{\Gamma(a)\Gamma(b + \frac{1}{2})\Gamma(b-a+\frac{1}{2})}.$$

Haunted and daunted by wanted
Jaunt halted, taunted

By bided byes now nullibieties,
No pieties, no pity, no witty

Ditties or dull eidola,
No aureola or holometabola more,

All the aliquots that head held,
Vast vaticities, vanished,

A shed no motes float
In or out of, its moat

No boat may beat, no scout
Flout, the rout o routes

O Charon or charms complete,
No repeats, depleted plot

The lot o P-brane and brain
Trained in on the non known,

Not the Tao o physics, that sick
Trick, pyx o the right

Wronged by unrung numbers,
Numbed burrs, birds

Unheard, words slurred,
The poetry o Poe untried,

"The Bells" held, unbeheld
The bees o being bearing

Air where cares fare,
Nary a dare rared,

No droll paroles for tholed
Woes, blows o phobias,

Swerves from verve to nerves
Served down to *hors-d'oeuvres*

Or *hors délai* and *lied*
Led on to unread rdread,

No spoor nor carbon but bone
To date with late tic

Talks, those he'd heed
And head to order working

As tabla *que habla* nabla,
Clocking dockings like Occam,

Come now, the how heard
Till the toll be told:

Behold what we become:
Home tome o O,

Time times O
Our lurid lord moored.

1. I must say that one can put together an awfully good-looking math presentation nowadays. The geniuses from the old days would have been amazed. Ramanujan was practically only armed with a bare space in the dirt, much like Pythagoras. The things he did once he obtained 'pen and paper' were astonishing. What could he have done with a computer? Oh well, those who are to come will see us as deprived and simple, too.

For now, even a fifth grader can understand this:

25	16	80	104	90
115	98	4	1	97
42	111	85	2	75
66	72	27	102	48
67	18	119	106	5

91	77	71	6	70
52	64	117	69	13
30	118	21	123	23
26	39	92	44	114
116	17	14	73	95

47	61	45	76	86
107	43	38	33	94
89	68	63	58	37
32	93	88	83	19
40	50	81	65	79

31	53	112	109	10
12	82	34	87	100
103	3	105	8	96
113	57	9	62	74
56	120	55	49	35

121	108	7	20	59
29	28	122	125	11
51	15	41	124	84
78	54	99	24	60
36	110	46	22	101

This cube consists of all numbers from 1 to 125. The sum of the 5 numbers in each of the 25 rows, 25 columns, 25 pillars, 30 diagonals and 4 triagonals (space diagonals) equals the magic constant 315.
                    -Walter Trump and Christian Boyer, November 13, 2003

159

super (pseudo?) sudoku
B.C. (before computerage)
K.R. did NYT crosswords
in pen

2. "See" LIGO's chirp, burst, quasi-normal mode ringing, exponential decay.

Rigmarole

لاله رخ

　Rookh the book, cook
　The look, rock the lock

O the role call no droll
Rigmarole *lo*s to parole

O etym, item o time
Primed to lime prestige

On the stage o maze o image
Minus magus fragment till flag

O unflagging drag, the lag
O what was once undunced

Announced and nonced to new,
Nouses us to use

O music as muse o amused
Refuge, fuse o ruses

Loosed in the look o loss,
O os glossed to close

Instruments, immanent *Dissonants*
In consonants, arcos o *portos,*

Nature mort aux mots,
Motes o floats o quotes

O quartz quartos sorted
To tropes o entropy, ens

Sent to ends o kens,
Those lenses o tense these sense-

*[T]he reader
confronts words
that, however
familiar, suggest that
another unknown
language lies
concealed in our
common tongue.*
-Jerome McGann,
*The Poet Edgar Allan Poe:
Alien Angel*

Less leeses o grief graph
As liefs fleet in feet

Scanned as ands add
O's blows below

The felt belted by the delta
Function, junction o ought[1]

$$\delta(x) = \begin{cases} +\infty, & x = 0 \\ 0, & x \neq 0 \end{cases}$$

And nought, the fraught knot
O neurons near the spheres

Past apastrons, sites astrocytes
Assist as wist lists

O listening glisten in synapses
Apt at agons o cons,

Ces sons pwned and zoned
In O voids as re·corded chords.

1. The Dirac delta can be loosely thought of as a function on the real line which is zero everywhere except at the origin, where it is infinite.

Prime Rime

Ex-men ken no when
Where airs fare squared

Routes o mute computes
To unnumb numbers unencumbered

By phone zones no tone
Leading reads to gleed

Heat in beats no tweet
Counts as account o chaunt

O the spheres in queer veers
From abience to audience o nonce

Sense whence mense commences
In thee as qi, key

To prime rhyme to time
Algorithms to rhythms o prism

Breaks that make Blake
Dances chances at glances

Into sand as grand strands
O ecstatic vatic somatics

Act to track abstract
Signs in sine lines,   जीव

Chords scored for soared
Ears as seers near

Thrones in O zone grown
Known blown bones.

Afterword

Jerome McGann

Jeffrey Herrick's Verse

Compositions of the Flying Hand

Trued verse de nature O unvantage blest
What toft O home o air o geste o presst.
from Sen, 千, せん [archival selfmark: Chihiro, 千と千尋の神隠し]

Between two words of a sentence there exists an infinity of other words.
Raymond Queneau, *Les fondements de la littérature* (1976), Théorème 7.

Though I have known Jeffrey Herrick the scholar since the early 1970s, the poet did not swim into my ken until 1992 when he sent me a small book of self-published verse, *Patterns and Fittings*, which he revised and augmented eight years later and published as *Patterns and Fittings in Zipangu*. With its cross-language allusion (via Marco Polo) to a mythic Japanese paradise, the title quietly announced what has been his great, preoccupying subject: Language "our Being's heart and home" -- a human or Earthly Paradise, as William Morris wrote, because it is the one place where we can keep being uplifted to remember how to "fail better" (Beckett).

In his moving meditations during the dark time of WWII, T. S. Eliot recorded his struggles with his language:

> Words strain,
> Crack and sometimes break, under the burden,
> Under the tension, slip, slide, perish,
> Decay with imprecision, will not stay in place ("Burnt Norton" V)

"And so," he writes in "East Coker",

> each venture
> Is a new beginning, a raid on the inarticulate,
> With shabby equipment always deteriorating ("East Coker" V)

Were you to extract a conception of language from *Four Quartets*, you would see how different Eliot's thought is from Herrick's, who pledges allegiance instead to Morris's bracing apothegm: "You can't have art without resistance in the materials". Herrick takes language as an amazing grace, not "shabby equipment", a trying and testing gift from the immemorial past in any present to every future. Because "our language condition" is to be "tongue-tied", as he has written in the unpublished "Introduction" to his 2006 volume *Valences*, we are as helplessly exposed as any lover trying to say what we want to say.

Recoiling from verse that seemed enspelled in the illusions of meaning rather than in love with simple truth, Laura Riding embraced prose as the more "telling" medium, a place to face "the common risks of language, where failure stalks in every word" (*The Telling*). But for Herrick it is the very profusion of illusion that makes poetry – or as he verbalizes it, "poetrying" – the more risky venture.

[P]oetry puts us to the flames, with no parole from paroles. And the masters make us savor that post-dicament, some, such as [J. H.] Prynne, with *nous* in full sway, some, such as Swinburne, with music in full play. ("Introduction", *Valences*)

"No parole from paroles" – that is to say, these formed and ably learned poems are all life-sentenced beyond any idea of a prison house of language.

> Socrates … called Love a sophist, where Sappho has "tale-weaver."
> The associations of this serve to set me off on my own lyre, exploring
> the lies and lays of loves. I sing under this sign, aware that no word
> really comes to us alone, and I trust that anyone willing to ponder
> poetry is also the sort who adores the OED almost as an ode, is one,
> at least, ready to slow way down, look things up, and embark back
> out into the verse head first.
>
> ("Introduction", *Valences*)

For Herrick the line between prose and verse is ultimately as perverse as the infinity of words moving fyttefully between any two words of any sentence. "No parole from paroles"; "post-dicament"; "in full sway … in full play"; "sophist/Sappho"; "set me off on/ embark back out into"; "lyre, lies, lay, Love"; "the sort who adores the OED almost as an ode"; and finally "embark back out into the verse head first". These are the *q.e.d.* of poetic expression where "The annunciation is in the enunciation. And the sentence, taken as a unit of thought, is our sentence" ("Introduction", *Valences*).

For Herrick, poetrying is the only game in town he wants to play his surprising music. He auditions for Eternity by "explor[ing] the world through language in which the component of sound is foregrounded" ("Sounding Out a World", *Patterns and Fittings in Zipangu*, vii). *De la musique avant toute chose* and withal that, the torqued talk of the languages of the world, "the weird of words" in all their particular combinations of combinations, no unsound conceptual selections to translate what is being read into something other than what is being expressly said, nothing less than complete attention to the unobtrusive mass of the *sing an sich*.

Punning never stops: "And I allude to nutter ludicity and uttered seriousness, an echo a choice *morceau*". More so: in case you didn't notice, we're on notice. *Lector – caveat*. No language is safe from, all language is saved in, these promiscuous raidings (readings): "I try to make poems in which the use of languages other than English reinforces the force of the sings". So Herrick chooses a shapeshifted gerund to label such profligate action: "poetrying", or "a conning, tuning, toning and orchestrating of contradictions (*Poetrying* 105). And he executes the action under the directive wordplay that is his book's title.

Echoing the form of the demotic expression "almost and then some", it takes on the form of a logical proposition, as if it were briefly declaring: "Given that Almost, Thence follows the Sum of Sings".

If you read the poems aloud you will hear Herrick's different types of poetryings in the lexicons, the syntaxes, and the usage he deploys. No semiotic form, however demotic, obsolete, or inarticulate, is forbidden fruit. Because the language operates phonetically, morphologically, and graphically (epi-, biblio-, and calli-), the actions are linguistically transcendental, i.e., they are open and permeable with respect to the poetryings of other languages and they are pervaded by unheard melodies (cf. Keats) and unseen seraphs (cf. Byron). While some of these are hardcoded in the texts, many others come in from elsewhere because they have open invitations sent out by the Language this verse is servicing.

In that context, the mathematical passages in his poems are especially striking and pertinent. Drawn in all cases from post-classical mathematics, they signal that Herrick's verse lives and moves and has its being entirely within a human world that Wordsworth longed for but, unlike Goethe, Shelley, and Byron, would not imagine. But for some spirits in the dawn of that Fourth Age of Poetry -- in America, Poe was the first -- the time had arrived. Shelley prayed to the West Wind that it would "Make me thy lyre, even as the forest is" and in *Prometheus Unbound* we see how the prayer was answered. Acting as an impersonal, eolian lyre, Shelley replayed the hydrogen and nitrogen cycles in the language of an English dramatic poem. It was a poetic feat timed to a time and measure that was, as Wordsworth had admitted, beyond him:

> If the time should ever come when what is now called Science, thus familiarized to men, shall be ready to put on, as it were, a form of flesh and blood, the Poet will lend his divine spirit to aid the transfiguration, and will welcome the Being thus produced, as a dear and genuine inmate of the household of man.
>
> (Wordsworth, "Preface, *Lyrical Ballads* 1800)

In Herrick's verse we have a poet acting as a wind-harp for voices blowing through our quantum world. Not so much the named voices, often famous, that he sometimes names, but the voices of *natura naturans* that humans re-nature and often de-nature. Like Isaiah, his lips have been touched – for better and for worse – with the burning coal of what Shelley called the "diviner day" of a scientific world, as fallen as it is Enlightened. He announced this in his 2006 collection *Valences* where poetic measures re-measure the capacity of any element – any Blakean "minute particular", any Lorentzian "free electron" – to form combinations with other elements. Where Wordsworth took on Enlightenment obliquely, Herrick's *Valences* take it on directly, "head-on,

> since it has moved from an epistemology based on Logos to a view now commonplace in the field of quantum mechanics that language itself is completely inadequate to represent or formulate what happens in that realm, that only mathematics will do. Paul Dirac's dictum "Shut up and calculate" epitomizes this perspective. I take this as direct challenge to poetry as the medium in which it is necessary to both speak up and calculate, with the enginery of reason and imagination as fully engaged as possible with our languaged condition.
>
> ("Introduction", Valences)

Contra Dirac, Herrick's headlong verse is declaring this: if you're serious about enlightenment you need something more constrained than pasigraphy. So in his verse Herrick is showing and telling us: "speak up and calculus" – call us, cull us, and calcul us (see Herrick's demonstration he titles "Calculus").

It's not just that sound predominates over sense, it's that by "foregrounding the component of sound" the verse short circuits one of the most traditional and misleading models for reading and understanding poetry: elaborate hermeneutic paraphrase, translation into conceptual prose equivalences (ethical, political, emotional, philosophic), as if the poem were a code that had to be broken so that its secret meanings could be exposed. If you go that reading route, do you have as frank and simple a reply to make to that frank, simple, and inconvenient question you might be asked and perhaps should have asked yourself: "Well, if that's what he meant, why didn't he just say it?"

Marianne Moore posed that problem for herself in her famous poem "Poetry", the first time in 1919 and the last in 1967. This is how "Poetry" begins in 1919.

"Poetry"

I, too, dislike it: there are things that are important beyond all this fiddle.
    Reading it, however, with a perfect contempt for it, one discovers that
        there is in
  it, after all, a place for the genuine.
     Hands that can grasp, eyes
    that can dilate, hair that can rise
      if it must, these things are important not because a

high-sounding interpretation can be put upon them but because they are
    useful....

The verse then took that opening move through a series of examples of the kinds of "things" – the kinds of language things – that are handled in poetry.

Returning to the poem and the problem in 1967, she wittily reduced her long poem of 1919 to three lines:

I, too, dislike it.
    Reading it, however, with a perfect contempt for it, one discovers in
    it, after all, a place for the genuine.

You can begin to discover the wonder of both of Moore's poetic performances by focusing on one easy-to-overlook word, "it". Note simply that in the first instance the word refers to "poetry at large and in general", all the poetry that has ever been recited, written, printed, edited, read, or interpreted. In the second, however, "it" has yet another object in view, the poem that Moore published in 1919 and titled "Poetry".

At the front end and at the back end, poetrying is about the pleasure and instruction ("miscuit utile dulci": Horace, *Ars Poetica* 143) that arise in acts of precise attention. Coleridge described that as the effort to "bring the whole soul of man into activity". Because Herrick, like Blake and Moore, judges that "the chief inlets of Soul in this age" are "the five senses" (*The Marriage of Heaven and Hell*), his verse works to bring the reader into acts of attention to language, the fundamental intermedium of mortal to mortal exchange.

The verse isn't a van delivering meaning, it's a demonstrative action.

"The hearth and heart of this is … in the saying of it, the singing…. The annunciation is in the enunciation" ("Introduction", *Valences*). And those actions are fundamentally jussive, optative directions rather than imperative commands. Readers are being given lessons in the geography of language from a fellow traveller, reports from a field where we are all living and moving every day. They don't tell you everything there is to see and do because the reports are too focused, too limited – which is also to say, too precise and minutely particular. So they issue invitations to curious readers to stop, look, and listen. "You come too" was Robert Frost addressing us in a jussive mood that is an American equivalent of Vergil's "doceas iter et sacra ostia pandas ("show the way and open the sacred portals": *Aeneid* VI. 109).

As they are composed, Herrick's poems don't ask us to explain what they mean but to determine how they work. Even a glancing look tells you it will take some effort to do that. It helps to read them once or twice any way you like, and then – because the sound components are so insistent – to recite aloud, as best you can, what you read. At that point you will have to decide: do I go on with this? How?

Take as a test of how to engage the fifth work in his series of roundels: "ᚠᛁᚾ". That title puts you on notice right away that certain elementary things have to be identified, like pericynthion, alu, anas, alveromancy, perhaps nous. There are many other puzzling features, like the small "o" and its big brother "O", and the odd phrase "Stimula simulars".

So begin with a simple list:

ᚠᛁᚾ: a runic inscription of uncertain origin and meaning but by "general agreement … among scholars [it] represents an instance of historical runic magic or is a metaphor (or metonym) for it" (https://en.wikipedia.org/wiki/Alu_(runic)). "alu" is its English transliteration.

pericynthion: the position closest to the moon of an object in lunar orbit.

anas: plural of ana, a scrap of information

alveromancy: the use of sounds in a ritual practice of divination

nous: common sense (and/or is it the first person plural of the French personal pronoun?)

Adding all that to what you already recognize in the language, you will see (and hear) a poem that's reprising (see line 7) expressions that have to do with the moon. You might even note that the roundel is a singularly apt form for delivering all of the poem's many recursions.

What about "Stimula simulars"? A little work will tell you that "stimula" is the singular imperative of the Latin verb "stimulare" (to goad or provoke). But "simulars"? That looks like a nonce word made up of Latin and English (simul) and Latin (ars). It's also a word that sounds like "similars". (Make of all that what you will when you can.)

In my case, focusing on that phrase broke open what I saw the poem was doing. It's a network of singing words whose principal character and sound is "o/O". More than that, its singings ride on a road of directive forms: croon, sing, Stimula, rune (here rune is primarily a verb, though not only a verb), ride, sieze (though if you pay attention this word comes through as both an imperative and an infinitive). The imperatives drive a series of infinitives (verbal nouns that have as well adjectival and adverbial effects): (to) sieze, to know, to come, to sound, (to) see, to perceive, to commune, (to) attune, and – mirabile dictu! – (to) true.

The poem is the execution of a formula – once called an act of divination – that is being handed over to its readers. The meaning, as Wittgenstein famously said, is in the use, and here is a demonstration for readers to learn from. The action of the poem is a revelation of how poetrying speaks truth (is that a meaning?).

Footnote on "O/o", perhaps Herrick's signature linguistic gesture: "O" starts as the form of an exclamation that Herrick has nicely glossed as "the sound of a recognition of cognition" ("Poetrying my Own") . It is reprised in a minor syntactic key, the cognate little "o" that the verse turns at times (or, of, on) to pull into the orchestration of a fetching spheral music that keeps playing all through this book.

Such verse is like nothing so much as a musical composition only asking to be played again. So take my elementary linguistic observations as finger exercises with the score. A complex set of very particular actions with the common sounds and senses of our world of language, the verse shows you lively ways of how to go on living there, in "the very world which is the world / Of all of us, the place in which … / We find our happiness, or not at all" (Prelude [1805] X. 627-629).

Or look closely at the poem "Calculus", operationally similar but a good deal more conceptualized than "ᚠᚱᚾ". The pivotal (and rhyming) words "albedo" and "alcedo" are especially important for bringing the conceptual relations of the verse into sharp focus. If you start from the volcano on Isabela Island (Alcedo) and the Latin word (alcedo), you will find your way to the proportion of incidental radiant light emanating from lunar craters (albedo) and begin to understand why both have much to do with "lalochezia" (look it up). To study how they function in the verse, readers are called to cull the notional relations resonating from those words.

Or track the syntactic transformations generated by the disposition of the verse and the torquing of various words (for instances, "that" as pronoun and conjunction, "calculus" and "prime" as noun and verb, "come" as noun and as a final verbal prayer). The game with the title word "Calculus" is particularly striking and directive for a reader. The poem uses it to call, cull, and calcul the "undumb" unknown values to "come" forth to presence from rhythmic sequences like the following: "Whys / That answer after wise laughter / That lunacy in euphony is cosmogony, / The gone come Om, / Reposed in prosopopoeia, that calculus / As calls cull us … To prime numbers to hum / Some sum o undumb come". Are you lost there, "halted without an effort to break through"? You should be, and so you might as well, like Wordsworth, say this to "your conscious soul": "I recognize thy glory" (Prelude [1805], VI. 531-532).

The book's final poem is another "Prime Rime" working to prime its poetic numbers to play various "Chords for soared/ Ears", Herrick's acoustic transformation of "sights for sore eyes". Gaming linguistic usages like that is nearly as prevalent in this verse as the profusion of semantic and syntactic puns, two of which punctuate this key (qi) passage's prison breaks and break dancing:

> O the spheres in queer veers
> From abience to audience o nonce
> Sense whence mense commences
> In thee as qi, key

To prime rhyme to time
Algorithms to rhythms o prism
Breaks that make Blake
Dances chances at glances
Into sand as grand strands

Grand strands of sand? You'll have to look into other places in this particular act of verse to hear the messages passing through its I phone's zones. Halcyon wings are flying over the world's most turbulent events, cursed lives, and deadened landscapes. (Is that a meaning?)

The action is played throughout in a verbal mood scholars do not formally recognize in English, the jussive, though it is as prevalent there as anywhere, it seems to me. Hovering between the imperative and the subjunctive, the attitude of Herrick's verse is urging but not urgent. ("The imperative mood commands, the jussive directs" (OED).

> This
> Way out, pleas, and donut
> Forget your valuables, as values
> Bank from knab to gab
> In lines that bear their own
> Cognation in cognitions of quillets
> Larfing all the whys

("Jussive Fruit")

Check out "donut" in relation to "Hohlraum" and "particle physics" and you'll be in the mood to love the entire set of genial instructions on offer here. So far as language is concerned, Herrick's motto is "nihil alienum a me puto".

> the f of the ineffable
> Starts stops that socket
> The buzz of zero over

To uwies that keep you
In Ur discomfort zone

When you read that don't think about translating it, think about the f-stops on a camera that takes pictures of ineffable wor(l)ds; just listen to the buzz of the word zero, recognize that "uwies" is a noncense wor[l]d made up from American "owie" and Australasian "uie" and that your original "discomfort zone" is a fun house where "A thing of beauty is annoyed forever" (Charles Bernstein, "The Truth in Pudding") and where a minor minah bird stands and delivers a call of the wild. And did you notice that tiny "o" at the end? That's the poem braking into its witty (Japanese) Period.

The home of the pome that tempts
Attempts to the poems at the end
Of the mined in mind, the minah
That stands descants and delivers
The runes of ruins, the cull
Of the vild in play pens₀

But there's one more thing I have to say about this kind of writing: that it's replete with what Alan Davies long ago called "private enigmas in the open text". However assiduously you search these works you will always rightly feel that something in the verse is always escaping, not your attention but your grasp. For weeks after reading "Jussive Fruit" I struggled with that title until I finally wrote to Jeffrey to ask what exactly he had in mind. He explained that he was playing with the phrase "Juicy Fruit", the artificial chewing gum flavor that Wrigley first marketed in 1946 and advertised to the public as "a fascinating artificial flavor" – a rhythmic phrase that Herrick here recalculated as "a fascinating artificial grammar", i.e., the jussive mood.

Really? I wondered! How was I ever supposed to see or hear that?

The moral of that little tale, I came to realize, was simple. It made a difference that it made no difference whether few if any readers could ever "catch" the "source" of the title. And it made another difference that made a difference after I learned about that enigmatic passage. To explain that, I give another little tale (let Socrates guide you through those sophistries; Sappho was a "tale-weaver").

Having similar difficulties with the opening poems in the "Almost" sequence, I spent a fair amount of effort on the word "almaz", which means "diamond" in Arabic and in other Middle Eastern languages Herrick is familiar with. I judged the word must be, if not the qi, then one of qi's incarnations ("immortal diamond"). I was certain I was on the right track when I recalled Randy Crawford's song "Almaz" (from her 1986 album *Abstract Emotions*) and after I had internalized the continuous "women to women" presences, especially artists, that pervade the "Almost" sequence. So off I went into that reign of atoms we call the internet and turned up two fascinating anas:

1. That the celebrated Ethiopian actress and dancer Almaz Hailie had recently died (2020).

2. That another Ethiopian woman, a refugee and storyteller named Almaz, settled in Canada where her tales of struggle and wandering were a featured presentation in the Toronto Ward Museum (https://wardmuseum.ca/frontline/almaz-toronto/)

When I read the museum's quotations from some of her narratives it was clear to me that the signal epigraphs in the first of the "Almost" poems were being lifted from this website or some other more primary source. The nomadic Almaz came through her wanderings with the conviction "that one challenge, one problem, one issue, is just one door in your life that is being closed but only you have the ultimate power to close all the doors in your life." I immediately thought of Dickinson's "The soul selects her own society", which Herrick might easily have taken as his watchword poem.

But when I wrote to Jeffrey to tell him of my research discoveries, he wrote back that he had never heard of Randy Crawford's song or of either Almaz. "I'm flabbergasted at all these coincidences I knew nothing of. My flubs leave me ghosted. Or, indeed, my soul selected her own society".

Most poets, even the most linguistically eclectic, mine the riches of relatively local deposits of language and commune directly with relatively restricted communities. Herrick began writing beyond the boundaries of Europe and the Western world when he left the United States in 1975 to teach at universities in Libya and Palestine and, beginning in 1981, in Japan, where he has since lived. From the early 1990s he has been writing verse under the horizon of the global internet, where the entire world has begun to learn to live, for better and for worse. So he writes out of his personal engagement with a world whose "center is everywhere and whose circumference is nowhere", as Medieval theologians liked to describe God. Hence all the private enigmas in his strenuously open texts. But hence too the flabbergasted possibilities of response that the Language he invokes has licensed and set free. The Language Herrick composes inside is so unimaginably vast in both its sounds and its senses that when he sets out to poetry with it, he inevitably calls and culls calculations he never took the measure of. But then we may see what he's singing about: that the Language already took care of what he was doing and what he was after, and of what we might want to do in response. Took care objectively, like the celebrated grace of a celebrated God who, it is said ("it"?), has the whole world in his hands. (Who said that? Nobody that we know of. And it wasn't "said" anyhow, it was sung – "as if that song could have no ending".)

Selected Herrick Bibliography

[Note: Herrick has released three CDs recording his recitations with jazz accompaniment: *Home Om* (double CD, 2016), Bill Coon (guitar) and Darren Radtke (bass); and *Anamnesis* (2016), with Bill Coon, Darren Radtke, Tom Keenlyside (flute) and Jun Kaji (keyboard). Five videos from these recording sessions are available under his name on YouTube. He also has several unpublished complete books of verse, including *By the Numbers, Lith, Oming, Omlessness, Skeltonic Tonics,* and *The Future o Literature*.]

Patterns and Fittings. Poems by Jeffrey Herrick (np, nd, privately printed in Japan in 1992)

Patterns and Fittings in Zipangu (Osaka: Tsune-Ato Shuppan, 2000)

Valences (Osaka: Tsune-Ato Shuppan, 2006)

Poetrying (Tokyo: Eishosha, 2011)

Home Om (Osaka: Noah, 2017)

About Jeffrey Herrick

guns → snug

After finishing my graduate studies at Chicago under Jerome McGann, I set out to let the world set me on fire. Having minored in Italian, I set my sights on a Dantean scene, but instead ended down in a hotter spot, Libya. I professed literature in Benghazi, then, fired up to proffer more of the pales of poetry to Palestinians, I panned to Birzeit, where I was fired upon by Israeli soldiers. Sufficiently burned, I left for Japan, a place with almost no firearms. At every rate, I have been in Japan ever since, snug with no guns pointed at me. (Not by the way, I have not forgotten how I was mugged at pistol point in Chicago and had shotgun pellets from pheasant hunters almost pelt me in a field in Utah.)

utter b → butter

I wear my influences on my leaves, my heart on my tongues. Any reader willing to sing along is also, perhaps, likely to read the reeds of Ornette, or net the horn of Om and call it home. And if that like sounds you, you may like to know that there is much more where *Almost   Thence   Sum* came from, largely unpublished, for example a collection titled *The Future o Literature*, one of 154 sonnets titled *Oming*, one of darker harks titled *Omlessness*, some satirical calls, including *Skeltonic Tonics* and *Anything you say…*, plus a 24 x 24 x 24 x 24 workout, *By the Numbers*. Then there's *Lith*, introduced here in the "Proem," a work including photographic evidence, ditto a new set of sonnets underway.

Be a B and utter these, please; the poems before you may well be butter or better on your tongue.

About Jerome McGann

Jerome McGann is a pedant (in the best sense, he says). He lives in Charlottesville VA, an historic American place that American fascists once tried to occupy. Like his namesake, he is devoted to scholars and scholarship. He has sometimes written verse, which he is certain always in the end aspires to the condition of Nonsense, which it sometimes achieves.